J'en El & Dr. O₂

JENEL@FindingComfort.com

Tel: 304.457.9771   Tel: 858.382.8211

Diamond Director – Million Dollar Club Member

http:VibrantHealth4u.usana.com

FINDING COMFORT IN YOUR OWN SKIN

– Reclaiming Your Authentic Self –

By – J'en El

Published in San Diego, California by Fortune's Gate, Int'l.
www.FortunesGate.com or www.FindingComfort.com
Editors: Lois Mathews, Michael Adamson, and Sarah Kendall
Consultant: Michele Blood
Library of Congress Catalogue Card
First Edition - printed Oct., 2002 in the United States of America
ISBN 0- 9722392-1-9 Self Help and Philosophy
To Order More Copies Of This Book Go To:
 www.FindingComfort.com or Call 800-567-3602

– DEDICATION –

To Mom and Dad, Bob and Gertrude Magid

- Thank you so much for your open minded, playful ways and assuring me that "There's *nothing* I can't do in life." I believed you!

To my grandmother, Rena "Bubby" Magid

- For showing me unconditional love and adoration. I really needed that!

To my Uncle Earle Magid

- For showing me how to be generous and kind…I followed in your footsteps!

To Oprah

- You've inspired me to overcome hurdles and leap into greatness. Now I'm able to move others to do the same!

To Werner Erhard

- Thank you for demonstrating integrity, how priceless it is, and for making it possible for me to embody it as well.

"I applaud all of you and celebrate your essence.
You will always live in the midst of my heart!"

– ACKNOWLEDGEMENTS TO CONTRIBUTORS –

As a result of being somewhat of a "Lone Ranger" my entire life, I was truly surprised at just *how much* assistance I needed in completing this book! I'm so deeply appreciative for the wonderful and extraordinary people who worked on the sidelines, cheering me on and being the wind beneath my wings! There are far too many of you to list here, as that would be a chapter in and of itself. You know who you are however, because we talked on the phone, exchanged emails, went to lunch, and attended meetings on a weekly basis. You are my life-long friends, and I want you to know how much I love and cherish you!

- The team that was divinely sent to me to see this book through to completion is comparable to none! There were "editors" who never edited; photographers who never snapped a photo before my prompting them to; and "illustrators" who never took an art course. All of you stepped into the shoes of excellence and worked within my time-line and budget just because...*I asked!* Bless you for that and so much more!

- To Michele Blood...my heart overflows with gratitude to you my radiant and extremely talented friend. Your ever-present gifted talents are endless. You are a true visionary who shines your light for all to see. You helped introduce clarity during moments of doubt. You assisted in redirecting my vision and harmonizing my thoughts with much love and understanding. You are a role model and an inspiration. Your experienced coaching and instruction were masterful and enlightening to behold. You were deliberate, delicate, and sensitive. That helped prod me to the next level of excellence. Observing you and learning from you provided me with the education I missed in school. I aspire to your level of distinction and quality. You show the human race what we all may yet be! I treasure your friendship, love and support, sweet sister of light!

My Editors: - To Michael Adamson...We have been together for nearly a dozen years. You have always gently and lovingly supported me in living my life in happiness without judging me. You are smart, funny, intelligent, and handsome, but more than that,

iii

you are my friend. You did the entire edit in three days even though I was "pushing the rope." You always step out of your comfort zone for me, and I appreciate you more than words could ever say. You are my man, my mate, my editor, my companion, my love and without a doubt, my best (male) friend! Thank you for encouraging me to be the best I can be!

- To Lois Mathews...You did a fabulous job! You put your heart and soul into this work. Your thoughts and ideas were brilliant. I'm so glad you're one of my dear friends.

- To Sarah Kendall...Your honest, practical, systematic, efficiency was so helpful. I'm ecstatic that you and your husband Gene Furbee are in my life.

Book Cover and Web Designer: - To Ang Dawa Sherpa...Dawa, you are a creative genius! I loved watching your talents grow before my very eyes. Your gentleness and open-mindedness bring a huge smile to my face. You are so fun to work with! If this was your first plunge, I can't wait to see what you give birth to and produce in the years to come. You're on a roll my sweet friend!

Hair Design: - To Christina Foucher...Girl, when it comes to hairstyles, you are a master artisan! You can make anyone look extraordinary and feel special. Thank you.

My Supportive Friends:

- To my *SOS Women's Group*..."Sisters of Substance," you contributed so greatly, with your visions, prayers, support, and cheerleading, as well as your faith and belief in me. You always knew my potential and you lovingly nurtured me through the entire process. You were my sunshine on cloudy days! I have no other words than...thank you and I Love You...Solluna, Ayesha, Mae, Ca'Brina, She'lah, Darlene, Mary, Myeka, Eleanor, Charmaine, Tashieka, Jaribu, Kathie, Kimmie, Frances, Patty, Victoria, Sharon, Gabrielle, Kali, Airya, Patrizia, Jean, Mehenta, Joy, Sheona, Erin, Iris, Charlene, Janey, Laurie, Felicia, Rosemary, Casey, Yvonne, Pat, Sunshine, Jacqueline, Le'Nora, Jacquie, Linda Lou, Laura Mc., Rain, Carol and Heidi's *HarMoney Cards*.

- To Aliza "Ali" Guggenheim...Girl, you were my guardian of insight and perception when I began writing this book! You are a brilliant woman and friend. I love and appreciate you very much.

- To Nadine "Yochelson" Miller...when we met in 1978, I think I learned what friendship could really be. That was the beginning of what I call the "enlightenment phase" of my life. From you I learned many powerful concepts of not only "how to be" but also "powerful words to use." Because of you, I became conscious of my vocabulary and how important in life our words truly are. Thank you for the gift that is "you," Nadine. Not even 3,000 miles can disrupt our friendship girlfriend.

- To Maggie Lancy...I'll never forget the day we met. It was 1994 and you were sitting behind me in a seminar. I heard your heart when you spoke. I knew I had to meet this live volt of electricity. "By chance" you called me the next day and you've been a significant part of my life ever since. You touch my heart and keep it filled with love, Maggito!

- To Kathy Roberton; Liah Holtzman; Pearl Ruben; David Oswald; Dr. Derrick and Sandi D'Costa; Justinn Tyler; Paul Schumann; and Lori Vogan Bell. I love each of you from the bottom of my heart. Thanks for being there for me!

If I have failed to mention anyone who helped me undertake and fulfill this task, please forgive this inadvertent shortcoming on my part.

– TABLE OF CONTENTS –

INTRODUCTION –

This is a GUIDE on "How To Find COMFORT in Your Own Skin!"

- Comfort leads to satisfaction.
- Satisfaction leads to gratitude and appreciation for what you already have and are.
- Gratitude and appreciation lead to feelings of fulfillment.
- Being fulfilled leads to pleasure, joy, peace, and happiness.

When you feel *gratitude* for what you have right now, you will find comfort in *who* you are right now and experience "more good in your life" as a result.

If you really want to find the solutions to your questions, **don't** just skim through this book. I've intentionally scattered *nuggets* throughout each chapter so that you would read the book in its entirety, rather than just *sift* through. Besides, as much as we'd like to wave a magic wand and have clarity, we must remember that our body, mind, spirit, and soul are not separate. Everything in life connects with everything else.

Listen to the CD, many times over until you achieve what you want. If you do not have the CD, please visit my website at: **www.FindingComfort.com** and order it immediately.

This is **not** just another self-help book to read one time and put away on a shelf to gather dust. It's an **action** book! Highlight your way to a new life! Do whatever it takes to flag your attention so that when you do actually re-read it over and over again, it will assist you in learning more quickly. Give yourself permission to own it now, as an investment in the new you! Make notes in it. Highlight all areas that speak to you. Underline, fold corners, and mark it throughout until it becomes yours. It **is** yours!

Experiment with and *experience* each *highlighted concept* until your life looks and feels the way that you always knew it could! Allow yourself to be responsible and own your life now.

By Transforming Ignorance... Clarity becomes Wisdom!

The importance of highlighting every word that *speaks* to you cannot be stressed enough. Because after you read through the book completely, ...then, on a daily basis, you'll be able to work on some of the highlighted areas until they become a habit. By doing this, you will eventually have the *quality of life* and *relationships* you've always known were possible!

Be patient and gentle with yourself. Take one tiny step at a time and you will gradually and successfully metamorphose everything that you don't like (or even loathe) about yourself into the person you've always dreamt you would be. You are *permitted* and *entitled* to a transformation that will override all stress and depression. It's okay to *allow yourself* to have it all!

This book contains tips on *altering* and *re-constructing* old habits, patterns, and behaviors. It will also assist you in achieving the desired benefits of effervescence, vitality, stamina, endurance, energy, strength, and/or power you've always known were possible! Remember...a habit is simply a traditional way in which you have become accustomed to doing something. If you learned something once, then you can re-learn an alternate way of doing it the next time around. This book is ultimately about becoming...the person you *choose* to be now.

It's said that it takes 30 days to create a new habit! If you begin today and miss tomorrow, don't beat yourself up: just start over again, taking one day at a time. If you miss a day, that simply means that you start at Day 1 again until you go consecutively for 30 days straight. Then, if you choose to stop after that, it's your business. Just make sure you *re-choose* everyday until everything in your life is designed by you and for you. Ask yourself...am I worthy to finally have everything I ever wanted? Yes you are!

I've invented my own Punctuation for all of my books. It's called *"EXPRESSIVE, CREATIVE, PUNCTUATION."* Since I write the way I speak, I believe in highlighting, sizing, bolding, italicizing, quoting, capitalizing, etc.

An English teacher might not be very happy with my "creative punctuation," however, quite honestly, I don't care! I believe in "whatever works" to get a point across! Expression and identification of specific terms are crucial for making certain points stand out. That is the point of this book!

Count on me to repeat important messages over and over again. Actually...to *affirm* something is to say it over and over again, until your subconscious mind gives it life.

NOTE: As I mentioned earlier, each chapter is not self-contained. The answers; how to; and *keys for growth and change*, will be woven throughout the pages and chapters of this book! Sorry, but there's not just one simple answer! There's work to be done on your part if you want to bring your authentic self to the forefront and find comfort in your own skin, as well as, make sense of it all.

You know...I'm amazed when people go to a doctor to treat or heal "just one part of their body," as if it's distinct and separate from their life's activities and level of stress. This is nonsense. We're complex components made up of numerous different aspects, ingredients and conditions. Our behavior, demeanor and attitude depend on all of the following:

- <u>Spirituality</u> can cover an array of religious beliefs, ideology, thoughts, convictions, philosophies, opinions, and points of views.

- <u>Emotions</u> deal with feelings, the senses, passion, compassion, sympathy, empathy, insight, understanding, and patience.

- <u>Psychological</u> is more cerebral and deals with mental, intellectual, rational, and irrational thinking.

- <u>Physical</u> deals with tangible, internal and external organs, and/or bodily functions. The physical aspect of life affects all of our senses.

Spiritual, Emotional, Psychological, and Physical All Overlap! They are a single continuum!

If we have stress, embarrassment, discomfort, disease (dis-ease), depression, lack of communication, disagreement, contention, animosity, dislike, malice, displeasure, struggle, strife, conflict, hostility, anger, etc., then chances are...we will make ourselves sick! We'll *create* dis-ease!

Since it took a lifetime to get to where we are right now, then let's "inspect" *who* we've become. This will give us insights as to *what* to "expect" in our future. This is a great place to begin our journey together. For if we are not *inspecting* what we are *expecting*, then we're probably already behind the eight ball.

My passion about *living life fully* on a moment to moment basis is what I attempt to do daily. It's been working in a way that has allowed me to enjoy life at a new level of *living from love in the moment.* I will share with you my formulas.

Personally, I've worked hard to build a reputation based on integrity. I've done this for myself, (and no one else). It's important to me that I wake up every morning *really* liking who I see in the mirror! It's pretty much about being the best I can be; about living out loud; about doing it over again every single day until I get it *right!* It's about caring. The "mistakes" we made in the past, were then! They just make us stronger to be better human beings for a brighter tomorrow. Today is a new beginning! Here's to you and your *New Life*! Here's to your *brighter tomorrow.*

LET THE JOURNEY BEGIN!

- J'en El

Playing at Life, Instead of Working at Life. Taking Charge! You can transform your life, FOREVER!

> *"For Where Your Treasure Is...*
> *There Will Your Heart Be Also."*
>
> *- Matthew 6:21*

We all know that our world has changed since the tragedy in New York on September 11, 2001. In fact, it affected the entire world. Most of us woke up in numb disbelief! Our collective consciousness took a turn on a grand scale, and the things that used to seem important, somehow just didn't matter anymore. The human perspective of what *really* matters changed almost overnight.

What owned us as a nation the day before (such as bills and job insecurity) became almost inconsequential. The only thing that matters now is taking charge of your life, enjoying yourself, uniting with friends, creating overall peace and harmony in your home, and being the best human being you can be... *always* with integrity and honesty!

Most of us began to ask..."What *really* matters in our final hour?" And..."What if our final hour is NOW?" "What holds significance?" Playing at life...instead of working at life! Taking charge of your life literally became more significant than any business venture or event. Humans have had yet another wake-up call!

Taking charge of your life *right now* became the most important choice. Personal contentment, serenity and gratification are now in the forefront. If you expect "magic in your nation," you must create it in your own body and your own home first!

But, what does it mean to take charge of your life? For everyone, the answer is different. But overall, it's feeling the best you can, every single day, for as long as that lasts! As a race, the overall questions became:
> ➤ What makes me feel good?
> ➤ Am I having "fun" right now?

> ➤ Do I have personal peace and harmony in my home?
> ➤ Am I making a positive difference in the world?

Taking charge of your life *right now* became and is…the primary choice.

This is where my book begins. I'm not a scholar, doctor, professor, or sage. I'm merely an empathic observer, philosopher, poet, and I love the human race. I simply care about people! My experiences are vast and I will divulge many discoveries and revelations with you. Since there were no instruction manuals, directions, blue prints, or guidelines for the perfect/flawless life at the time of our birth that I could refer to…I decided to create my own. I wrote this reference guide to assist us on how to happily co-exist with the outside world, how to shed old habits and beliefs, how to metamorphose into the people we'd like to show up as today, and how to find comfort, peace, and a growing sense of well-being in our own skin.

One thing I learned over and above anything else is to enjoy every moment of every day to my best possible ability. As you read this book you will conclude, solve, or discover how to do the same.

Most of our parents (God bless them)…just didn't have a clue! They're human! They did the very best that they could, given the information that they had available to them at the time of our birth and formative years, just as their parents had.

By default, facets of our ancestral heritage were integrated into *who we are today.* The only chance we had was by trial and error, or, to learn from someone else's mistakes, (probably by watching the Oprah show). She's been a positive pioneer of opening Pandora's Box of *issues* that were hidden away and remained secret or taboo far too long.

A few years ago, I had to literally *re-invent* myself. I just wasn't having fun at the game of life. I intentionally contrived my own demise! I shed my old beliefs that were no longer working for me. A new…"Designer Me"…emerged. It took work on my part, but I had nothing to lose, and everything to gain. Anyone can do this! There was simply no more room for paranoia, insanity, jealousy, and blame. I had to take a stand for my own life. The best place to start:

- Get rid of the *fear*...but how?
- Get rid of the *pain*...but to what end?

Ridding myself of old *traits* and *beliefs* was imperative, and a great place to start! CAUTION...you may grieve the loss of your old "useless habits" along the way on your Journey of Self Discovery. One thing is clear...to get the *results* we must do the work.

- You may desire more abundance.
- You may want to be more loving.
- You may wish to *feel* more peaceful.
- And...you may wish to *know* love *and* joy.

Each of us has had at least one painful inquiry that we've needed answered throughout our lives. Most of us have been searching for an answer. If there were even a slim possibility that even just one of your concerns about self-awareness, self-control, self-confidence, or maybe even self-mastery is addressed in this book and tape series, wouldn't you read it? I would; I have; and I still do!

For me...life became about making *every day* special! Let this book guide you *into a journey of self-discovery*, and inspire you to have everything exactly the way you ever dreamed it could be. Keep reading, and I'll share with you in a clear, easy, concise way, the most fundamental and essential *benefits of listening to the heart*. You *can* transform your life, FOREVER!

Here are some of the topics that we'll cover...

- How to resolve issues that have been holding you back
- How to live out loud
- How to contemplate inwardly
- How to reclaim your wisdom
- How to withdraw to a "secure place"
- How to reclaim your power and energy, by using nature.
  (Instead of draining the life force from others.)
- How to embrace your spirituality.
- How to increase stamina.
- How to live passionately.
- How to express your sexuality.
- How to create results for a new you.

- How to connect with others of like- minds and always attract
  the right people at every moment.
- How to take charge of your life by identifying old characteristics
  and belief systems that were created "for you" by your ancestors. -
How to reduce conflict.
- How to reduce stress.
- How to release depression.
- How to rest, re-new and rejuvenate.
- How to effectively ask for what you want, and get it!

I'll offer recommendations on how to *design* a new life, so that all of
your tomorrows will give you a smile of contentment, peace, joy and
satisfaction. I will steer you in the direction of listening to your
heart, in making wise, clear, concise decisions that will support your
inner peace, as well as help you recognize *your qualities of
distinction* over time. Remember... *clarity* leads to *wisdom, and
wisdom* leads to *empowerment*...your own Power!

Allow this book to be your key to having everything you ever
wanted in your life and more! Use it as your personal guide for self-
awareness. It will require *work* on your part! Nothing in life is free!
Ask yourself if you're worth it. If not, put it down now and walk
away. If so, jump in, and never look back, for your old habits and
old way of life will no longer be an option!

Life... How glorious it can be.
Appreciate what you already have!
It's time to "wake up" to your Spirit.
It's time to "wake up" to the Love of "yourself."
Life wasn't meant to be hard.

Don't simply "tolerate," but rather
Be flexible and *allow* "who you are" to just be.
Give yourself Permission to be part of the living.

Examine your Thoughts
Are you saying..."Yes?"
Are you saying..."I can?"

Before we can have peace in our world,
It must reside in our heart *and* home,

Take charge of your Destiny...
Claim peace, love, harmony, and prosperity
Now!

      - J'en El

In A Perfect World...
You can be Happy and Successful on a Daily Basis!

If opportunity doesn't knock, build a door.

- Milton Berle

When I began writing this book, I had a scenario in my mind of what it would be like to live in *the perfect world.* Actually...*my* perfect world. I wanted to solve the problem for not only my own pain, but for the universal suffering, discomfort, agony, and distress that underlies *daily,* almost every news article that appears on a minute to minute basis.

I actually want all humans to have, joy, peace, and inner harmony. We've each heard the cliché that all peace starts from within, but unless you *feel* that peace experientially, then it's nothing but words and hot air. Simply *reading* about peace unfortunately doesn't automatically give you the *actual feeling* of it. Sometimes there's just a lot of hard persistent work that goes into finally finding it!

I positively took what I believe are the necessary steps to create and design a perfect world for myself. I stopped working, (even though I was in debt.) I could no longer let money take charge and rule my life! I began to wake up to my biological clock instead of using an "alarm." I also tried to floss on a daily basis (which seemed next to impossible). I strive to exercise 3 to 5 times per week. (You'd think that would be realistic in a perfect world).

I dreaded "Mondays" so much, that I began to make it my *special day,* to do anything I wanted to do. I looked inside to *feel...*"What do I *really* want to do today?" After a while, "Mondays" weren't enough, so I decided to make Tuesday through Sunday, *special* as well. You'd think I'd be able to have a smile on my face continuously after taking charge of *every day.* That should have pretty much covered happiness on the "Richter Scale of good times." After all, it only makes sense that in a perfect world, we'd all be able to wake up to *ideal* conditions and have it remain that way 24/7. Of course, it would be appropriate in an ideal world for our weight to match our size and body frame. As an added bonus,

10

feeling naturally invigorated during all waking hours would be the final feather in our cap. And, finally...to have our perfect mate by our side would be the ultimate.

Now...Let's have a Reality check!

The bad news is that I found more obstacles in *my perfect world* than I ever could have imagined. My *designer world* began crumbling before my very eyes. It just wasn't perfect, no matter how hard I tried. For a while, I was delusional! Something was missing. I was sure there was no *perfect world*. Even with my newfound freedom, I still got bored at times. I had too much time to *think*, rather than *do*. The truth was, I never really knew what *I* wanted to do when I grew up. I only knew what my parents and teachers taught me.

I realized at age 50, I had never really had *an original thought.* I recognized I was so busy *trying to please people* my entire life and to do the *right* thing that I never knew *what* was *right* for me. I found myself *thinking* so much that my favorite new adage became... *"Stay out of your mind...it's a very dangerous place to visit."*

My negative thoughts were dull and boring. They defied and contradicted any "good things" that I ever dreamed about for my own well-being and/or, any potential future of happiness. What was I thinking? Actually, I wasn't, and that's where my problems began. I was so *conditioned* during my rudimentary years that I don't believe I even knew it was okay to think for myself.

I finally had to surrender to the fact that the *only* way we could live in a perfect world was to be *grateful* for what we already *do* have. If we compare or look outside ourselves and to circumstances that occur around us...we lose! We must *always* look within to see and feel what works. No one else can tell you what *works* for you...so don't allow them to!

Of course, in life..."stuff" happens! It's how we handle the "stuff" that really matters. Life is a process, a smorgasbord if you will. Life is nothing but an array of *choices.*

What I found in my search is that it's so very important to make and take the time to delve into your inner world, to find out *who* you

11

really are, and to find out *what* you really like to do! We actually need to go in search of *our authentic self.* In doing so, you *will* find peace. You know you've come home to yourself when you become comfortable in your own skin. Eventually, I was able to distinguish *my* thoughts *from* my parent's thoughts. I was able to differentiate my likes and dislikes from theirs. That's when "true freedom" really began. That's when life became fun. Read on and find out how to put these same skills into action for yourself.

I remembered hearing a long time ago that if you take care of your self *first,* then everyone around you will be taken care of as well. In my mind, there are a few glitches to this presumption. Since I now have my own point of view, my interpretation is that if we treat ourselves *at least* as well as we treat others, then maybe we've all got a shot at inner happiness.

This book's intent is to help you create the best possible world for yourself. To assist a few lucky people who will actually take and make the *time,* to put themselves as a priority. To make your self #1, maybe for the first time ever. And...

- Find Your Authentic Self
- Learn how to feel at home in your body.
- Learn how to fine-tune your attributes.
- Learn how to put your skills into action.
- Learn how to re-invent yourself.
- Appreciate what you do have.
- Actually like yourself.
- Understand your roles in life.
- Get *personal* with yourself and find out what
  you truly like to do!

Also...to discover for yourself *who you are really,* and the role you are meant to play in this world.

There's a *peace* that comes in knowing *who* you are. There's a *calm* when you allow your true nature to be in harmony with your words, thoughts, and actions. This book will help you learn who you *really* are so you can happily co-exist in the world, and quench your desires.

– HOW DO YOU LIVE YOUR DASH? –

I read of a man who stood to speak at the funeral of a friend.
He referred to the dates on her tombstone from the beginning to the end.

He noted that first came her date of birth and spoke the following date with
tears; but he said what mattered most of all was the dash
"we live" between those years. (1934 – 1998)

For that dash represents all the time she spent alive on earth...
And now only those who loved her know what that little line is worth.

For it matters not, how much we own - the cars...the house...the cash.
What matters is how we live and love and how we spend our dash.

So think about this long and hard...are there things you'd like to change?
For you never know how much time is left, that can still be re-arranged.

If we could just slow down enough to consider what's true and real,
And always try to understand the way other people feel.

And be less quick to anger, and show appreciation more,
And love the people in our lives like we've never loved before.

If we treat each other with respect, and more often wear a smile...
Remembering that this special dash might only last a little while.

So when your eulogy's being read with your life's actions to rehash...
Would you be proud of the things they said about how you spent your
dash?

- Jackie Barrinough

Having fun is not an option...it's mandatory!
If you're stuck in a job you don't enjoy,
I bet there's a better job for you.
The older I get, the more fun I want to put into my dash.
If it's not fun, I won't do it.
Let's start putting more fun in our dashes right now!

- Wally Amos

13

Authentic Requirements:
Find the Qualifying Factors that set YOUR Personality apart from MINE.

*We've reached the moon
And then returned,
But we find it troublesome
To walk across the street
And meet the neighbors.
We have conquered "outer space"
But not our own "inner space"*

- J'en El

I coined the term *authentic requirements* to get people in touch with their *individuality.* Authentic requirements are simply various *unique components* that make us individuals. These components distinguish my personality apart from yours.

If I wake up today, and do what I *feel* like doing, instead of what I'm *supposed* to be doing, I would most likely be at peace, and feel extremely content...not to mention ALIVE!

If we lived in a perfect world, it would be simple to think this way. Unfortunately, most of us were blessed or cursed with *guilt,* and we operate out of obligation, burden, and fear. That's when the vicious cycle of disharmony, discontent, depression, stress, and disease usually begin. Our lives become so filled with *responsibilities* that we lose sight of what we're really here for. We're so busy *doing* that we're hardly ever *being.*

It is my intention to aid you in getting in touch with your authentic requirements and unique components. Learning to say *no* to others *without the guilt...* is a great place to say *yes* to your self! This will assist in creating *your* most perfect possible inner world.

To some, it may sound selfish to put themselves first. I've done enough personal experimentation with inner peace however, to feel like a *master* on the subject. I constantly have to ask myself...

14

- What are *my* requirements for happiness?
- What makes me feel good in life?
- What do *I* want to do today?
- What do I do that makes me feel like I'm my own personal best?
- What will it take to *have it all*?
- How bad do I need to hurt before I do something else?
- What price am I willing to pay, to *feel* good, *do* good, and *be* good?

My answer became... *change*. Change everything about myself. Actually... to have it all, I had to *re-invent* myself. Change the way I think. Change the way I look at things. Begin *listening* to "what others have to say." *Listening* can be a lot of work! The end gain is definitely worth it however. Why would anyone wait until they hit "rock-bottom" to change? The one main determining factor for people not to consider change is that they do not *hurt* badly enough yet!

I know that some people never will be willing to do what it takes to have it all. Personally, I would consider this to be insanity, sabotage, and self-destructive. Having your own needs met is vital to having a *successful* life. I use the word *successful* as being triumphant over adversities. The *mind* is one of the biggest obstacles to overcome.

I'll be writing a lot about the *mind* throughout this book. The mind represents all those tiny voices that speak to you constantly. It's a nagging reminder of all of the negative undertones we've incorporated into our subconscious over time. This is why *positive affirmations* are so important. An *affirmation* is something you repeat over and over and over again. It is a statement that "confirms a belief" or a pattern we hold in our subconscious mind. Affirmations can be positive or negative. It's your decision to choose what to tell yourself. Because your subconscious mind is subjective, it believes *everything* you tell it. So, why not speak to yourself *positively*! Repeat affirmations over and over again and always state them *in the now*, such as...

- "Miracles are happening to me right now and everyday!"
- "I now have more money than I'll ever need or require!"

I will be elaborating more about this in the chapter on "affirmations."

Check in to see what you're telling yourself on a daily basis? What words do you use? I've learned to be very careful in differentiating what I call the *spirit/heart voice*, from *the antagonistic rebel voice*. It took me years to listen deep from within and clearly know the difference. Once you learn to distinguish the mind-chatter, you can travel to new levels within yourself.

As I learned to listen to my inner spirit or heart voice, I realized I was not using my time wisely. I was a workaholic and put my needs, dreams, and desires on the backburner! For too many precious years, I chased after the almighty buck! These days, I make the time to *check in with myself,* thereby doing what I love to do, instead of "someday isle." My friend, Dr. Denis Waitley says to "follow your passion!" Denis wrote this piece many years ago, and it's my privilege to share it with you now.

"SOMEDAY ISLE"

There is an island fantasy
A "Someday I'll," we'll never see.
When recession stops, inflation ceases,
Our mortgage is paid, our pay increases.

That *Someday* I'll where problems end,
Where every piece of mail is from a friend.
Where the children are sweet and already grown,
Where all the other nations can go it alone.

Where we all retire at forty-one,
Playing backgammon in the island sun.
Most unhappy people look to tomorrow
To erase this day's hardship and sorrow.

They put happiness on "lay away"
And struggle through a blue today.
But happiness cannot be sought
It can't be earned, it can't be bought.

16

Life's most important revelation
It's the journey that counts...not the destination.
Happiness is where you are right now,
Pushing your pencil or pushing your plow.

Going to school or standing in line,
Watching and waiting, or tasting the wine.
If you live in the past you become senile.
If you live in the future you're on Someday I'll.

The fear of results is procrastination.
The joy of today is a celebration.
I've saved, and I've slaved, trudging mile after mile,
But I'll never set foot on your Someday I'll.

I paid all my dues and put in my time,
And out of nowhere came another Mt. Everest to climb.
From this day forward make it your vow,
To take *Someday I'll* - and make it *now!*

-© Denis Waitley.

Reproduced by kind permission of *The Waitley Institute.*

Ultimately, making time to do the things you love allows you to be creative and enjoy life in every moment. When you give yourself this kind of quality time on a regular basis, it allows you to learn *who* you are and *what* you want. Time to get in touch with your very own basic, authentic requirements. This is what allows you to be *unique.*

We all get to make it up every day in a new way. Just like the movie *"Ground Hog Day."* Personally, if I get to live another 50 years, you can bet that I'm gonna' do it *authentically* at the heart level this time around. It's never too late to start being truly happy. Allowing yourself to revolve your *lifestyle* around your *personality* is a relief, because you finally give yourself permission to live a contented life with ease and comfort, which offers a freedom to really live and love life to it's fullest everyday.

If you re-read the last few paragraphs, you'll see that it's a cycle. Once you begin the motions to take charge of your life, it will take on a force that will intensify your actions to *bring you home*...home to a place you may have *never* been before. Your questions are always answered when you listen, and follow your heart. The answers are always amongst the debris, just waiting to be discovered.

Since there's only *now*, we may as well forgive ourselves for past mistakes (even though I don't believe there *truly* are **any mistakes**). We must learn from our lessons, and start having fun. Begin to have fun *right now*!

We all know that we can't control what happened in the past, however, we *can* control our actions *right now*. Ultimately, all we can really do is be responsible for this very minute. We all start with the same number of seconds, minutes and hours every single day. What I finally had to resign myself to is...there really is *only now*. Surrendering to this moment allows us to live in the present. That's when time ceases to exist! That's when everything starts to make sense and fall into place.

My partner used to say "Stop trying to push a rope!" The *effort* will not only make you very tired...it's futile! To effort at anything in life is exhausting. He told me to *relax*. I used to get angry hearing those words. It took years of deep introspection to really get the meaning of what he was trying to tell me which was to simply *be* in this moment *as* this moment!

He was right! Life doesn't need to be hard. We all have so much input every single day here on earth. Why contribute to that insanity?

My book became *not* about a perfect world, but eventually evolved into living each minute as if it's my last, and feeling great and comfortable while doing so. That's when "living in the *now*" made sense. Being comfortable with *who* I was to become, was made easy through complete surrender. To assist in our surrender, we can use many methods that I speak about throughout this book.

You'll find more information of the techniques to use, in various chapters on the following procedures: Yoga; deep breathing;

isometrics; weight and resistance training; and aerobics just to name a few.

Words just can't describe how valuable these exercises are. You must *experience* them to fully understand just how much they will contribute to your well-being. Don't fall into old habits and rip yourself off! Remember...Do the Work, because finding comfort in your own skin feels so good and you *are* worth it!

I've begun to see life as a huge puzzle with many pieces scattered about. If we all start with the same exact puzzle, the difference would be in...which piece we pick up first. Wherever each person begins conjoining *their* distinct puzzle actually determines which direction they personally take in life.

Every time we put another piece of the puzzle in place, another question is answered, and/or another question may arise. The reality is...each individual question is answered at a different time for each of us. That puts us all on a different page. There is *peace* in surrendering to where our pieces have landed. It's okay to surrender to where you are, and, at the same time... *take action now* to remedy your tomorrow. To make it the best possible life, moment by moment, day by day.

If you want to change your future, you must consciously choose to let go of suffering, anguish, and bitterness. We can stick our head in the sand...or we can deal with situations as they show up in life. The quickest way is by clearing the mind and then replacing negative thoughts from our past with positive thoughts through meditation, writing and affirmations. We **must** give up what *isn't* working! After all, would you rather be right...or happy?

<u>Meditation</u> allows you to clear and quiet the mind. It also, helps develop your powers of concentration, visualization, and imagination to assist in formulating, transcending and going beyond the muck and gloom that has held us back for so long. Meditation allows for a fresh, perspective and awareness for new things to occur.

<u>Writing</u> allows us to get in touch with our heart's dreams, goals, desires, beliefs, possibilities, and potential. Writing also enables us

to "change our attitude" leading to new perspectives about our lives, and what we really want to do with them.

Affirmations allow us to clean up the negative mind chatter that we've fallen heir to since birth.

- "I am always divinely guided to be in the right place at the right time!"
- "I choose to live in the now, trusting life will show me how!"
- "The perfect people are always magnetized and attracted to me!"
- "I trust in life to guide and carry me away to my highest good!"

(For more, see my chapter on "Affirmations.")

It's good to be thankful for all of the suffering we've experienced in the past, for it has brought our consciousness to a place of desiring to search for a better tomorrow. After all...how could we know *good* without having experienced *bad*?

If your life and future could be changed for the better, with just one minor adjustment, wouldn't you find the courage to make it happen? As I look back in time at my own activity, I see life as a pendulum. It began with a far swing to the right, then a far swing to the left. Experimenting every step of the way. When the pendulum returns to the right, its "swing" is not quite as far as the first movement. When I return to the left, it's also *not quite as far* as the last swing. Back and forth, right and left, until one day I felt centered, balanced, and at peace. We literally "inch" our way to *change*. Adjust each move until we get it right. Right for you! Maybe not right for anyone else, but remember...It's *your* life. Only *you* know *where* you're supposed to be and *when* you're supposed to be there. All you have to do is continue to *check in with yourself!*

Are you doing what you love to do? Eventually, if we listen to our heart, a new, natural rhythm will begin. Not something learned, but something magical and bigger than our mind.

Let's talk about how to *experiment* with the *Pendulum Theory.* As I mentioned above, it's extremely important to keep "checking in" with yourself. By that, I mean to honestly evaluate your feelings after each action or interaction you participate in. This is not hard to do. You simply see how you *feel*. If you become nervous, upset or stressed, you're probably off track! If you feel happy, fulfilled, centered and balanced, you're probably on track! By doing trial runs of "what works" and "what doesn't," you will be saved from a lot of grief and aggravation in your future.

Let's explore our *communication skills* (or lack thereof). There was a time in my life, when I felt like everything I said was *wrong*! I was beginning to feel like a child, learning to speak all over again. It seemed like people were getting mad at me and misinterpreting every word that came out of my mouth. I was getting extremely frustrated, as my livelihood was even at stake. I started to experiment with different phrases and ways of saying things with kindness and compassion, instead of *demanding things with arrogance*. Surely there must have been a way to ask for something without demanding it, as if what I was asking for had been *owed* to me.

I was in such a quandary about *how* to speak, that I felt compelled to let people know I was working on my communication skills and to please bear with me during my moments of transition. I asked for feedback and made notes, until eventually, I am now able to communicate in an effective way without trampling on anyone's ego.

One of my more painful lessons, was when I began to learn that when it comes to *egos*, we need to know ahead of time that some people really feel the need to be *right* all of the time. We must remember that most wars have started because of the *attachment to* different points of view, and certain individuals feel the need to fight or argue, rather than to know that maybe everyone's accurate, and there's never a need to fight or argue over anything. We simply see things in a different way.

If you ever feel as if you are banging up against a brick wall, just get clear *what's right for you* and walk away if you need to. Some people argue for their limitations! Stay true to yourself without being righteous. Righteousness can be extremely ugly if something

21

is being forced down your throat against your will! I've found that kindness works best, whenever possible. Also, you can suggest what has worked for you in the past, as opposed to *telling* people what to do. This will most likely keep the peace, as long as no one has *attachments* to the outcome being a certain way. Having expectations and attachments is another chapter entirely.

Having *no expectations* is part of living in the moment. Having *no expectations* usually just makes life more enjoyable for you and everyone around you because it's hard to be disappointed when you expect *nothing*.

In searching for inner-peace and happiness, sometimes we look outside ourselves...to others, to help soothe our pain. My experience is that *to go within* by using deep breathing, meditation and relaxation techniques, really helps to clear the cobwebs for a clearer thought process.

Getting oxygen to the brain and cells of our body aids in minimizing and alleviating stress. It helps clear our thoughts, which lead to a feeling of inner-peace. Remember...stay out of the mind, it's a dangerous place to be! It's like walking through a minefield full of untapped explosives.

Whenever I feel nervous, tense, sensitive, upset, defeated, agitated, angry, worried, or have low energy, I better know to walk away and breathe deeply. Try it! It brings a sense of balance, and feeling centered. Breathing stimulates you to the core, and helps you reach the depths of your soul! It can bring a sense of *calm* like you've never experienced before. One of the latest techniques that I use on a daily basis which only takes about a minute, is to walk outside and find a *power spot,* (a place which has "my name on it,") where I can breathe in the life force of the trees and plants and birds. Breathing in nature, in this way, is like plugging into an electrical socket and being charged by the power of the universe, without the negative side effects of electrocution!

Because trees and plants and birds are alive and natural, you're actually breathing in the life of a higher and balanced power source, which brings light and clarity to anyone who does it. If I get a negative phone call or feeling, I walk outside immediately. If I'm driving down a road and have a negative thought, I just *plug into the green of nature*, and life becomes favorable, instantly! Anyone can take a minute of his or her time to feel great! Remember...You're worth it! Don't ever give anyone the power not to let you take a moment for yourself. It's simply re-charging your cellular batteries! This is vital to everyone's well-being!

Some people turn to drugs or alcohol to find comfort, consolation, escape, or relief, or even to numb themselves from *feeling their pain*, or *facing their fears*. I believe this is like placing a bandage to hide or cover up, our feelings, rather than dealing with issues as they arise. We can run, but we can't hide from our issues. Until we grant ourselves the favor to stop, experience, face issues and forgive all involved, (including and especially) ourselves from getting into certain situations, than nothing will ever be healed or resolved.

The journey we choose to take which contributes to our *recovery* will allow us to give back to society in numerous ways. We get to be a *representation of numerous possibilities* that can occur in the universe. Alternatives that we could not even fathom beyond our wildest imagination.

We all, as individuals get to say *what's so* in or about our life! I am convinced that *agreement* is a key ingredient of people's beliefs. Here's an example. We're at a party, and we're very good friends. I introduce you to Mary, an out of town guest who's been my friend for years. In my introduction, I tell you that "Mary is one of the finest and most generous human beings I have ever met. She is kind. She is wealthy. She travels the world. Mary has several estate homes, which are quite lovely.

She is an entrepreneur with at least 10 multiple streams of residual income, but will probably never even have to touch that money, because her Trust and inheritance is so huge, that she couldn't possibly spend all of her money, even if she lived for many lifetimes."

I guarantee that you would believe every word that I speak about Mary! And, not only would you believe me, but you would then, turn around and build up Mary saying the same things, until everyone in the room, "knew" who Mary was. By *agreement*, Mary would be all of that and more!

If this is actually the case, that I could make all of this up about Mary (and, I promise you that I did), then just about everything in life is a function of *agreement*. To drive the point home, let's consider a different scenario.

I am about to introduce you to Gina. Before Gina enters the room, I tell you she's turned to prostitution to make ends meet financially. (This is not really the case, but I just don't like Gina!) So, when Gina enters the room and I introduce you, you already have a preconceived notion of *who* she is, *what* she does, and probably have lots of *judgments* because of the gossip and dirt I spread about her. No matter how wonderful Gina may actually be in *real life*, she will never have a chance to show how wonderful she is, because I dirtied the slate before she ever knew what hit her! Actually, in reality, Gina is the wealthy one, and Mary is the prostitute. But it doesn't matter, because by *agreement*, they are *what* and *who* I said they were...to which you probably agreed.

If *agreement* really is this powerful (and it is!), then you can see not only how important it is NOT to gossip, but also to say wonderful things about everyone, especially to yourself as well as to others. As a matter of fact, not to say anything at all, unless you have something good to say! There absolutely is *agreement* in the world that whatever we say becomes a reality.

If you want to be rich, affirm it by speaking and writing, the following affirmations:

- "I am a magnet to money in all forms!"
- "Money is my obedient servant!"
- "I now have time to achieve all of my true goals and I am debt free!"
- "I am a magnet to money, I now have more than I need!"

If you want to live in the *Perfect Home*, affirm it with the following affirmations...

- "Where I live, exceeds my dreams, and I own it debt-free!"

- "Perfect housing and my income always exceeds my needs!"
- "Where I live is spacious, beautiful, calm and serene!"

The truth is, people don't know who you are until you show them or tell them. You can re-create and re-invent yourself at any given moment. It's all, ultimately about *agreement.* Actually, when you say so, things begin to happen, and not a minute sooner.

If *what we say* truly makes that much difference and I believe it does, then "affirming the positive" simply makes sense and is a wise thing to do!

Some of us will hold on to the pain and suffering of our past, maybe because it feels so familiar. What you are *familiar* with however, is not necessarily always the best. What do you think would happen if you started saying *good things* about yourself, instead of perpetuating the negative?

Since it takes only 30 days to change a habit, this makes room for all kinds of miracles to show up in our lives. If the pain is intense enough and the possibilities real enough, with a little direction, coaching, and insight, we are all able to gravitate out of the quicksand into the light. Peter Pan said... *"With one happy thought, I can fly!"* Begin to greet each day with love in your heart, for miracles are always at your fingertips, just because you say so!

I received the following email many years ago. We could all learn from this story. How do you perceive yourself today?

– A Woman Looks In The Mirror –

Age 3: Looks at herself and sees a "queen!"

Age 8: Looks at herself and sees herself as "Cinderella," "Sleeping Beauty"

Age 15: Looks at herself and sees herself as "Cinderella," "Sleeping Beauty," "cheerleader," or if she is "PMS'ing": sees "fat," "pimples," "UGLY"...(Mom can't go to school looking like this!)

Age 20: Looks at herself and sees "too fat/too thin," "too short/ too tall," "too straight/too curly" but decides she's going anyway.

Age 30: Looks at herself and sees "too fat/too thin," "too short/ too tall," "too straight/too curly" but decides she doesn't have time to fix it so she's going anyway.

Age 40: Looks at herself and sees "too fat/too thin," "too short/ too tall," "too straight/too curly" but says, "At least I'm clean" and goes anyway.

Age 50: Looks at herself and sees "I am" and goes wherever she wants to go.

Age 60: Looks at herself and reminds herself of all the people who can't even see themselves in the mirror anymore. Goes out and conquers the world.

Age 70: Looks at herself and sees wisdom, laughter and ability. Goes out and enjoys life.

Age 80: Doesn't bother to look. Just puts on a <u>purple hat</u> and goes out to have fun with the world.

*We should all grab that purple hat a little earlier in life.

<u>**Everyone needs to be told they're great...so here's to YOU!**</u>

To an exceptionally beautiful person!
Your beauty is not in the clothes you wear,
The figure you carry,
Or the way you comb your hair.
Your beauty must be seen within your eyes,
Because that is the doorway to your heart,
The place where love resides.
Your beauty is not in a facial mole.
But true beauty is reflected in your soul.
It is the caring that you lovingly give,
The passion that shows with passing years,
As you grow old!

...YOU *ARE* BEAUTIFUL!

- Unknown

Let's face it, finding "inner peace" is different for everyone. Personally, I found true transformation is in the "pure heart of innocence." Innocence begins at birth and typically lasts until one goes to school when and where judgment and indoctrination begin. There's no need for innocence to *ever* end. *Innocence* simply means purity of heart, the inability to hurt and be hurt. *Maturity,* on the other hand, means fully developed or reaching one's prime of life. This is exciting because it means we *never* have to give up one to have the other!

To make sense of why most adults lose touch with their innocence lets take a trip into the past to see *how* and *why* innocence is covered over and when it all began!

Innocence Regained... Taking A Trip down Memory Lane. When and where it all began!

Everyday that you live is a special occasion!
- J'en El

I still remember the awkwardness and insecurity I felt as a young child. There was always someone watching over my every move. Did they have expectations of *what* I was supposed to be doing? I had no idea. Maybe that's why I like to be alone so much as an adult. I don't need someone watching over my every move. Especially when I'm playing! Understandably, there are hazards that can jeopardize the health and safety of a young child, but overall, if you're not specifically *teaching* something important, then there's absolutely a certain amount of *space* that human's need, regardless of their age. I simply wanted to be left alone...not hovered over! I felt plagued with what felt like *expectations* from the elders who watched over me. Talk about confusion...the adults wanted me to do *everything* "their way."

Sometimes, it felt as if I were watching my life unfold on a giant movie screen. I had *no say* in anything. The pattern of *trying to please* got old very quickly. By the age of 5, I felt like an idiot! What was the point of God giving anyone a brain if you're not allowed to use it? By this point, *my lack of understanding* had obstructed any possibility of happiness.

Finally, when I became a young adult and started my singing and speaking career, I continued to have the same sick feelings of queasiness I experienced in my youth. It was always *as if* I were missing a piece of the puzzle.

Looking back, I can still tap into the feelings of inadequacy and vulnerability that were to become my reality for far too many squandered, depleted years. I was missing a piece of vital information, and I was determined to find it, no matter how long it would take! Fortunately, I was to find out very quickly however, precisely, just how much *authority figures* impact our lives. Whether knowingly or not...parents, teachers, family, and so-called friends literally mold and subject us, as children, into the images and expectations that suits *their* needs and desires. What gave people the right to try to vicariously live their lives through ours, as if we were sacrificial lambs?

Therefore, I had to ask myself... *"Who am I really? How much of my being is authentic and how much is simply the programming of others? Where do they stop, and where does the real 'me' begin? How do I rediscover and reawaken the creative side?"* I don't believe that we need to wait until we're senior citizens to figure it all out... let alone get it *right*.

As adolescents, we are dependent and impressionable. I specifically remember acting out *learned responses* to accommodate the people I loved whether the responses made sense or not... just like a robot. In looking back, I believe most of those responses came from *fear*. They were essentially programmed responses that made no sense at all. When you're living in a fear, desperation, or "survival mentality," you do what you *think* you need to do just to get by... or even survive.

As I matured, I began to understand that *who* I become depends on the *choices* I make in life. This helped clear up a lot of my uncertainty. From a dark abyss, the choice of *who* I was to become... became my journey of self-discovery.

In my youthful innocence, although I didn't understand the ways of the world, what I did know, was that I wanted to be loved! The demands I had instilled in myself at an early age eventually manifested as "self-inflicted expectations of perfection." This is too heavy of a weight and burden for any human to carry... *especially a vulnerable child!*

It took years of hard work to *change the patterns* "of giving over my power to authority figures." As a child, the only things that seemed important were to accommodate adult authority figures by doing whatever was necessary to obtain the results they needed to make them happy. It was all about *approval!*

What I finally was able to create, after years of constantly working on myself, was a resilient, vibrant, powerful, intelligent, lovable, grateful, passionate, and compassionate woman of substance. Today, the difference is that I know I have *choices.* I now understand the law of cause and effect. This understanding has given me the confidence to trust my decisions, knowing that I am responsible for doing what I want...whenever I want, as long as I am aware of all possible outcomes. To me, that means keeping my integrity level impeccable and maintaining personal responsibility at all times!

One of my happiest moments was in finding "my voice!" Learning to speak in public, *without fear.* The good news is that *faith* and *fear* can't live in the same place at the same time. The key to becoming comfortable in speaking to crowds of thousands came from the following lesson.

When you speak to people from your *heart,* rather than from your *head* (which in essence is speaking to people rather than at them), remember that you are simply having a conversation! How can anyone get nervous or self-conscious by just having a conversation with another, or others, regardless of the size of the crowd? When we learn to listen...we naturally know what to speak about. When you listen, you and everyone around you enjoy meaningful conversations.

Of course, *fear* will occasionally be triggered in your life. But I've learned that we are *never* put into any situation unless we already have the resources to handle whatever comes up! That alone should give us faith. If faith and fear really can't live in the same place at the same time, and we choose *faith,* which means to trust or believe, then we are always living in a *positive* "contagious" condition! Learning how to choose and manage your *reactions* to situations is critical for getting through circumstances quickly, rather than dragging them out for life.

There are many ways to expand our minds. Of course we learn through maturity and experience, however, there are other tools we can use to break through our barriers more readily. Using the following "tools" will make life more enjoyable for you and everyone around you: Books, audio cassettes, videos, CDs, DVDs, life coaches, affirmations, etc. All of these can speed up your learning curve, so **do the work!**

If you're not sure where to begin, walk in to any bookstore and browse through different sections. When you find topics that appeal to you, begin to skim through the books. You will always be drawn to the perfect publication that is needed to take you to the next level of your life. With modern technology, it's just as easy to stay home and shop online at various websites and stores.

Learning how to dissolve your fears and tap into your passion can eventually help create the person you *choose* to be. You can settle for scattered and unpredictable energy, or, you can "train your butterflies how to fly in formation."

Let's find out where *your* passion lives. Keep reading and you'll learn how to reunite with your heart and piece together the puzzles of where to find your *authentic passion.* Was it stifled at a tender young age, along with your enthusiasm and desire?

Do you even remember what your dreams were? Did you have any dreams? Or, did you buy into other people's ideals, images, goals, and fantasies? Those people who struggled but couldn't seem to manifest on their own, and yet, lived vicariously through you.

What will the *stimulus* be that finally ignites your urge to bypass the "old learned programming" in order to seek out your authentic passion, to live your life out loud fully, joyously, and consciously in each and every moment? Is it your turn to locate and honor that *life force* that's been buried away far too long? Only you can answer that question!

Rediscover Your Authentic Passion...
And understand your body's language!

If you don't take action now,
You probably never will!
Forget about "One of these days I'll,"
And make your "someday" now.

Our parents' taught us to the best of their ability. Like their forefathers, they attempted to arm us with all the necessary *equipment* to function safely and as happily as we could in a dysfunctional world. Unfortunately, part of their limitations were that most of them were living in *survival mode* and never had the time to seek out or live their own authentic passion.

As if that weren't enough, we were also genetically imprinted with our *entire ancestral history.* Unfortunately, we can't override all genetic imprints, but the good news is that *habits can be changed,* no matter how unnatural it feels at first. Some habits may take longer to change than others, however, once we recognize that it's *our choice* to change, it becomes easier to incorporate those very changes into our lives.

It was necessary as newborns and children to acclimate ourselves to our parent's world of expectations in order to survive in *their* world. Our minds had to function like sponges, busily absorbing the information as fast as we could, never knowing, and never questioning the validity of each program being downloaded by any or all authority figures. In time, this information became not only unconscious, but unquestioned and unexamined as well.

When puberty struck, we had already accepted the training and practice, like computerized robots, never examining it for distortions or accuracy. Needless to say, this input tremendously influences our adult lives and the way we function in the world.

So...what were you told? Were you lucky enough to hear... *"You can accomplish anything you want in life?"* Were you lovingly encouraged? Did you believe it? Or...were you one of those less fortunate ones who was *negatively* reinforced...<u>and, did you believe the lies</u>?

Our body, mind, and spirit respond to its environment. From the language we hear, to the physical gestures, as well as our intuition.

Negative comments can create anticipation, panic, desperation, depression, apprehension, extreme agitation, and fear.

Positive comments can create an unstoppable, self-sufficient, self-reliant, independent, competent, confident, well-adjusted human being.

How do you measure or identify the truth for yourself? Authentic Passion is equivalent to *always* doing what you love! You *always* know when you're *"happy gauge"* strikes 100%. Your interest peaks. You lose track of time. You stop watching the clock. You're aroused from your core. When you ask yourself *"What's RIGHT for me?"...* your heart always tells you what you like and what you don't. So find out what "fits" you!

You can *force* yourself to do just about anything in life, but merely going through the motions is not what I'm talking about. I'm talking about core heart desire. Keeping your *mind* out of it. That's the little *nasty* voice that manipulates and confuses you. I'm suggesting that we always listen to our heart when we want to find our truth. Our passions are most *aroused* and *awakened* when we act on our special inner voice. That's the spirit voice that gives you the big "YES!" If you have *any doubts* about whether or not to do something, then you **don't** have the big "YES!" Your heart will sing out joyously with positive, happy, feelings of delight, and you will clearly know you're on the right path. IT'S THAT SIMPLE!

Only when we do what we love, can we truly claim our power and feel the drive, strength, and force from within. This is what helps measure and identify our own truth of where our authentic passion lives and its true source. My experience is that people who take care of themselves are able to give to others more freely, joyously, lovingly, and abundantly. Why? Because they have something to give!

When you feel *centered* and *balanced* and doing what you love (at an interest level of 1,000 % plus), then you can bet that the origin of your achievements came directly from your heart, and that you are living, walking, and breathing your authentic passion, unquestionably! Anything less than 1,000% level of joy and satisfaction is veering you off course and away from inner-peace, happiness, and quite simply…your life! Gauging and measuring your enthusiasm is very easy. Simply check in with yourself. How do you *feel* when you're doing what you love? How do you *feel* when you aren't?

Learning the hard way is such a waste of energy. What end result do you want?

Don't do anything that's less than 1,000% of your passion…Just don't do it!

- Of course, <u>be responsible</u>.
- Of course, <u>be reasonable</u>.
- Of course, <u>be appropriate</u>.
- Be sure to *always treat yourself* at **least** as good as you treat others!
- Don't *ever* answer the phone if you're not in the mood to talk to people.
- Don't upset the balance of your home (meaning your body) …Your body is your *palace*.
- Respect everyone's *space*…including your own:

I make an effort to spend quality time with myself everyday. I love spending time with me. One afternoon, I was in the kitchen, feeling great, having a perfectly wonderful time. I was really enjoying my special music, which was blasting on the stereo. I was cooking for the first time in weeks, having a fabulous time, when all of a sudden my mate came home and starts hanging out in the kitchen on *my* time. Then, his 21 year-old son came in and also started hanging out in the kitchen, *in my space…on my time*. They made themselves very comfortable, which definitely broke the flow of my fabulous afternoon alone, so I chose to leave the kitchen area and find another sacred space, which turned out to be the bedroom. This time I was smart enough to put a "do not disturb" sign on the door. Do you think they got the picture? Of course they did!

Do whatever you need to do to *have your privacy.* Also...take your *down time* very seriously, whether it's 5 minutes or 5 hours each day! Remember...we either have our "excuses or results" in life! I always do my best to *alert* my family in advance when I'm engaged with myself. Everyone in my family knows not to take it personally. I simply say I'm going to meditate now, and I won't be answering my phone or taking any calls! I've made my life more important than minor disturbances. People in my life now get to do the same for themselves, without guilt. Ultimately, we all have more respect for one another because we emerge as better, clearer, happier, more desirable people to be around, and when we do finally get together, our *special designated time* is *quality time.*

If you're not enjoying you're own company and your life...Ask yourself...Why Not?

- If you're feeling stressed or irritated...Find out Why.
- If you're feeling sad or melancholy...Find out Why.
- If you're feeling great...Find out Why.
- If there's a scowl on your brow...Find out Why.
- If there's a smile on your face...Find out Why.
- If there's a gleam in your eye... Find out Why.

Investigate, examine, and keep touring the depths of your heart. Pay attention to your needs. Listen to what makes you feel worthy, exquisite, whole, and complete. Find out what's feeding your soul and lifting your spirit. Continue visiting those places on a daily basis. Delve deep! Allow yourself to *let go of all the old negative input* that you've dined on for so long.

We all have *patterns* or *obsessions.* Some work for us. Some don't! Pay attention to your needs. Pay attention to your body. Pay attention to your life.

As I've mentioned before, there are many techniques and affirmations that will allow you to go deep within...methods that will allow you to tap into the deepest levels of your heart. I can't mention enough, how important it is to *get oxygen to your cells.* There are numerous ways to do this. Oxygen will affect your attitude and help with generating positive thoughts. Breathing deeply and continuously is one of the quickest ways to get to the truth…your truth!

I always listen to Michele Blood's songs, which are affirmations she wrote and put to music. What a powerful, dynamic way to liberate your soul. Her tape series and books bring about permanent, behavioral change, because you're hearing the message, combined with music. It becomes a part of you forever!

I can be driving down the street and singing her songs over and over, not even realizing how I am subliminally re-writing my script and changing my thought patterns. Here are just a few of Michele's songs. Be sure to visit her website: www.MusiVation.com and order her life-changing products. Her work is a must for anyone's self-improvement library!

THIS DAY

"I greet this day with love in my heart.
I am living this day as if it was my last.
Today I begin a new life!
Today my life has a new start!
I greet this day with love in my heart!"
*(The melody that Michele puts this song to is so sweet!)

BORN RICH

"I was born to live this way…I was born rich!
I was born to live this way…I set my goals today!
I was born to live this way…and rich I'm going to stay!
Cause' I was born rich!"

These are just 2 of the many fabulous songs that helped change my patterns and attitude to seek a more positive and fulfilling lifestyle. Sometimes I'll exercise to her tape series and sometimes, I'll meditate to her *Magnetic Creative Visualization Imaging* cassette or CD. Wow, talk about healing and cleansing!

When you hear her beautiful voice, singing and *affirming* over and over again to soothing, soft music, you can't help but change your thinking for the better. I'll be mentioning an array of products throughout this book, which will guide you to be the best *you* that

36

you can possibly be. These products will allow you to enjoy life in a completely new way.

I recently met with Terry Cole-Whittaker in New Mexico. Listed below are just a few of the positive concepts she spoke about during her lecture.

- Greatness means to be who you are!
- Know that this is your life to live as you choose!
- The power of affirmative repetition!
- 3 strikes and you're out is *not* the rule of God!
- Dare to be great!
- Set *realistic goals*, yet *always* reach for the sky!
- It's okay to make mistakes
- Resentment and blame stops the flow of creativity!
- Inspire people to greatness!
- It's what I think of myself that counts, so "nominate your self!"
- We have great roots and heritage since our father is God!
- Get over the limited thinking of yourself and others!

You've gotta' love Michele and Terry! They think BIG, POSITIVE, POWERFUL, DYNAMIC THOUGHTS! They help change people's lives. They make a difference!

In chapters to follow I'll cover in more depth and details the techniques I've personally used to break out of the mold and instill peace into my life.

Listen to your heart more often! This could mean simply staring into space and breathing deeply for a few moments, or it might involve taking a week off work, or sitting by a river for who knows how long. It may even mean something as extreme as quitting your job. Be responsible...but do what you need to do for yourself.

- *Think* a plan through.
- *Write it down* and be specific!
- *Draw a Roadmap* of where and how you want your life to go.
- *Do* the work.
- *Don't* be lazy with yourself.
- *Write* you're short-term goals first. What do you need to happen

immediately to begin molding your reality into what you want today, *tomorrow,* and *next week?*

- *Write* the way you want your life to look next year, in three years, in five years, and even ten years

Be REASONABLE! Also...be OUTRAGEOUS! Remember what Terry Cole-Whittaker said *"Don't set realistic goals...reach for the sky!"*

Expect what you imagine! Nurture your thoughts and dreams and never give up! Live each day as if it's already happening. Remember that Rome wasn't built in a day. At first you might have to start slowly. That's okay, because every step forward is a step toward creation and results for yourself, no matter how small of a step you take! Have what you want. Go for it all!

I've talked about *affirmations* briefly here, but it's important to go to the chapter on affirmations and do them everyday. You *are* so "worth it!"

> *Be good to yourself!*
> *Nurture yourself!*
> *Love yourself!*
> *Examine your life.*
>
> *Adjust your life with subtle, gradual changes.*
> *And, live out loud!*
> *...Everyone will benefit!*

Rent the movie "Ground Hog Day" even if you've seen it before! Watch Bill Murray do everything over and over and over again until he gets it right. Re-live each day of your life until it's *your best day ever!* Then, do it over again, *even better* the next day! Unless you're hurting another human being in the process, there is no *right* or *wrong* when it comes to *living your passion.*

Always be grateful for what you *already* have, and, at the same time, make sure you believe that you're worthy and deserving of more. Your thoughts are infinitely creative!

"Conceive and Believe in order to Achieve."

Living your passion is different for everyone. The only way to *gauge* your personal passion is to constantly be in touch with your feelings. Your truth in one moment may not necessarily be your truth in the next moment. Things change. Keep checking in with your self and make adjustments along the way. It's okay to revise your script whenever you wish.

How many times a day do you find yourself *happy?* What happens when you're involved with a hobby that you love...time flies! If your life is feeling dull and boring, then maybe you need to delve deeper. What if *anything* was possible? The key is to start living now, as if everything is possible! I've never heard of anyone who regretted living his or her dreams!

One of the most important clues to living your passion is to be in touch with your body. Everyone's body has it's own language. When you learn to understand your body's language, and *take action on your needs*...you win! To reunite with your heart, you must follow your bliss, and everything else will fall into place.

Our bodies speak in the language of *symptoms*, which show up as signs, traits and characteristics. We need to *prioritize* what specifically needs attention at each and every given moment. The challenge is to read the symptoms before they manifest and display themselves as a full-blown illness or disease.

Be sure to read and re-read the chapters on Food; Diet; Exercise, and, The "Real" You...Looking in the Mirror Naked!

Put "LOVE" into every moment and into every little thing you do!

Stagnation or Growth?
You <u>can</u> advance to be ANYTHING You Desire!
...STOP listening to the Dialogue of Your Mind.

> *"Even if you're on the right track,*
> *You'll get run over if you just sit there."*
>
> - Will Rogers

We all have spirituality!
...Some of us are just suffering from spiritual amnesia!

When I sat down to write this book I was more naive than I ever could have possibly imagined. I actually had the notion that I would complete this book within a few days. As the pages filled, so did my mind. Sometimes it felt like I was loosing my sanity. Some of my thoughts seemed absurd, some foolish, and some were even preposterous. The rate of information my mind had to process was astounding. It's said, *"When you're ready...the teacher will appear."* I just wasn't nearly as prepared as I thought I was.

I was soon to find out that everything in life is a *process.* Everything we do is designed to take us to the next level. This is a good time to touch on my explanation of the learning curve, which is discussed in my *Pendulum Theory* in Chapter 3. Fortunately (or unfortunately), there's either *stagnation* or *growth.* It's either up or down, but...there's no sideways. My few days of writing, turned into a fourteen-month marathon! It became a major event and ordeal! But in reality, it's still going on. The mind hasn't stopped.

The growth that we experience however will last a lifetime. Think about it...because we are continually passing our knowledge on to others, for generations to come, people will receive the information that we bequeath our children and the world!

Everything we do and say will be passed on from generation to generation, so it is for this reason that we must now take full responsibility for *all* of our words and actions from this day forward! Taking charge *now* will instantly give you a new sense of purpose in your life!

The point is, sometimes we "fall heir to *victim thinking*" because we let *our minds* temporarily be bigger than we are! If we *allow* our true desires, passion, belief, and faith to carry us forward however, then the *perfect people* will always show up in our lives to give us or to exchange the correct information that we need to get us to *the next level.* This requires a lot of faith! Once you begin the process however, your growth will take on a rate of speed you never would have imagined possible! We must *never* give up on our dreams!

The thought occurred to me for a brief moment only, that I could *give up* on my dream of completing this book. Why? Because no one would have known or even cared...*except me!* I quickly realized that if I stopped writing, the stagnation process would set in all over again and displace my soul unless I immediately reclaimed ownership of my life.

I looked up the definition of *stagnate*, and I knew that decay, rotting, and/or disintegration was simply not an option! That would have been like allowing the devil to devour my spirit and very essence. Whatever thoughts I had of giving up, instantly vanished. I was not willing to sell-out my dream of completing what I saw as my *"life's work,"* my creation of love...my first book!

There's always a *price* in life for getting what you want. It's simply a matter of *what you are willing to give up* in order to get what you want! Since we're all already busy 24-hours every day we must be willing to give up something. What about you...what are you willing to give up...Television; sleep; a job; a meal; a relationship that's not working? You get to call all the shots in your life. Maybe you could take a bus to work, so that you can have time to read. Maybe instead of going to a restaurant for lunch, you sit in a park and breathe consciously. Only you can answer these questions of what makes you feel good, and what price you're willing to pay. Only you can make the final decisions that will change the outcome of your life story.

41

As I began to do things that make me happy, I realized just how much I love life, how much I care about humanity, and just how much I do want to share myself with the world. We need to know, however, that not everyone is ready for what we have to say. I believe there are many "light workers" on the planet. I think of a light worker as a celestial spirit or angel, who is committed and devoted to perpetuating...Love; Gratitude; Appreciation; Recognition; Acknowledgement; Abundance; Generosity; Sufficiency; Cognition; Insight; Perception; Discernment; Non-Judgment; Instruction; Education; and Awareness.

I'm uninhibited and awake enough these days to say that I consider myself a light worker. I believe there are many of us on the planet! You know who you are...no matter how humble or unassuming!

I used to take so much for granted. I had to learn to *become* grateful. I would thank God...for everything, but I was just giving lip service by saying the right words. Until I met with others who were really less fortunate or had a poverty consciousness or deficient attitude, I didn't *really* realize just how blessed I am! I've become so appreciative of everything I have these days. I do believe that *gratitude for what we already have* is vital to attain happiness every day. I saw that it was impossible to move from unhappiness *to* happiness until I'm already honestly grateful for the way things are and the way things aren't. I need to know that it's already perfect the way it is!

When I sit in my backyard, I'm actually in love with the grass and the flowers and the trees, and the energy they provide. I *really* used to take all of that for granted! I choose to enjoy life and have fun today, while I'm still here on the planet. Suppose this really is our only time around? Suppose this is our last day on earth?

My point is, if I gave up on writing this book, I never could have experienced the kind of growth and gratefulness I've encountered and discovered to date. Today my life feels like an adventure! In my wildest dreams, I never could have imagined the kind of feelings that would be stirred within my soul, just because I allowed myself to do what I wanted to do. If I had quit, I never would have known or felt this sort of accomplishment or satisfaction in this lifetime. I may as well have been dead! Living with apathy and dispassion was just *not* an option for me. Ask yourself what changes you need to make now to turn *your life* around.

It seems the less I write on my calendar, the more of an adventure life becomes. This way, I get to *make it up*, everyday. I never really know what I'm gonna' do. That's the truest form of freedom I've ever experienced. Give yourself permission to experiment. Write on your calendar to take a week off, *by yourself...* and **plan nothing!**

Since we get to choose every second of every day which path we want to take. Find out what turns you on and go for it! We *always* have the *choice* to do what we love!

Give yourself permission to remove the clutter from your life and get organized. Rid yourself of everything that's keeping you from reaching your goals. Fill your schedule with the things that bring enrichment, joy, and satisfaction to your soul, rather than filling your life with resentment by doing things you know you dislike.

There will always be times in life when we're just too tired to do certain things. We need to honor that, and rest. To do absolutely *nothing* is essential at times! Listening carefully to our *spirit/heart voice* will always keep us clued in to naturally know when it's appropriate to relax, or when we need to take action and grow.

Give yourself permission at any and every given moment to do what you need to do, whether that means to remain idle for a while OR grow! Always remember to keep listening for the answers *and* solutions, for they are constantly changing!

The resemblance of life to a garden is amazingly parallel. Have you ever stopped to *watch* a garden grow?" If you've ever tried to *see* a tree sprout overnight, you know that it's not possible, unless you use time-lapse photography. When we plant a seed, all of the optimism in the world won't produce immediate results of maturity or fruition. Like our lives, *it's a process.* Flowers, trees and plants, (like people), gradually progress from birth to death, requiring water, food, and the appropriate nourishment, love, and care.

In nature, we must learn what each individual, or seed requires...sunshine, shade, (or both); daily or minimal watering; an identical plant to cross-pollinate with, etc. We all know that yielding of results takes time, and are different for everyone and everything on the planet. Nature takes its methodical course. Everything has a proper balance and cycle. Illness, disease and death will always occur sooner or later, so why not just be, do, and have the best of everything during your short stay here on this planet?

I labored at learning *patience,* for it was never one of my strongest attributes. I had to work hard at learning that *results* take time to show up. To me, most processes that I've put myself through seemed immeasurable, but with patience and persistence, I learned that *results are inevitable!* If we *create a plan,* take *action,* and give nature time to take it's course, we'll ultimately, see the desired outcome. Planning *and* taking action are the *key* words here.

I don't believe there's any such thing as an overnight success, or a free ride in life. We all pay our dues in one form or another. Whether we pay with money, time, or experience remains to be seen. But paying with *lies* always creates damage, harm, and pain! I think that *lying to yourself* is one of the quickest ways for a human being to impair their growth because the choices become fewer and fewer.

Lying to yourself starts out as a protection mechanism, but ultimately it backfires and puts you into a corner with fewer and fewer honest choices that you ultimately could have made for yourself. This is why it's so good to *think things through* before taking action. But, think quickly. There's no need to drag out your life. Sometimes an opportunity is only for the moment, so we must use our instincts wisely.

The minute you become inattentive or neglect your needs (by not nurturing your soul) is the very moment you've allowed yourself to become a harmful, desperate, careless, and reckless human being! In life, there's *always* a chain reaction! Your neglect is a sure guarantee that everyone around you will be harmed and suffer in one form or another, by your lack of consciousness! Sooner or later, you haphazardly, thoughtlessly, or circumstantially, will create damage, merely because you've lost sight of who you really are, or what you really want to do in life.

Just by not being in touch with *your* truth, can create havoc in all of the lives around you. We're talking about spouses, children, parents, friends, co-workers, and the list goes on! I think the cost is way too high. Taking time to pay attention to your desires, cravings and needs, is a favor you need to grant yourself and the world! It's simply common sense. It's paying attention to what your heart is really *begging* for. *Listening* to that little inner voice is vital, for it *always* ultimately leads us to the place we're supposed to be in life. Taking action on what the voice is telling you to do will bring inner peace, love, joy, harmony, true health, and happiness.

> *"Anything you want to ask a teacher, ask yourself.*
> *If you really want to know the truth,*
> *The answer will meet your question."*
>
> - Byron Katie

If you ignore the voice of your heart, you are living with one foot in the grave! The cost to everyone, (including your self) can be extremely devastating, not to mention exhausting! Until we listen to that voice, and make the necessary changes that need to be made in our lives, we are living a death sentence! We always have a choice, whether to feel lost and depraved, versus living our chosen path. Once you've chosen *your* correct/given path…the old ways and habits are no longer an option and begin to lose their strength and become obsolete. You become free from old beliefs that held you back, when this occurs.

I had a facial at 1:00 pm on a Wednesday afternoon. My mood was *really great*. When I checked my cell phone for messages on this peaceful afternoon, I was told that my house was broken into and valuables were stolen. There was a fleeting moment of feeling intensely angry and violated but I decided it wasn't worth upsetting the harmony I was feeling just moments before. I chose right then to continue on my path of balance and peacefulness. Just because someone else was a jerk and a thief, why should I give him the power to affect my mood and state of mind? What's done is done.

45

All we really have left is what's next…right now, Right Now, Right NOW! We need to keep BREATHING!

The bottom line is that we're always gonna' have to make choices in life. Chocolate, vanilla, and 31 other flavors. CHOOSE! If you don't like Chocolate…choose again. By re-choosing, our lives stay fresh and enjoyable rather than stale and stagnant or always feeling like we *have to* do this or we *ought to* do that.

Initially, we may make choices that take us down paths that don't always serve us. This doesn't mean that we're *stuck* with our choices. This is where self-correction comes into play. We can change our plans, thoughts, and actions at any given moment, for no other reason than because *we said so.* How grand it is to know we can keep doing things over and over again until we get it right. It's back to that movie *"Ground Hog Day."* I keep choosing to do my life over and over again, until I get it right. "Right" *is what feels right for me!* REMEMBER to keep checking your integrity level and be responsible for your actions in all choices and changes you make…especially if it includes other people.

Another gift you can give yourself and others is the freedom to *speak from your heart.* Think about how good it would feel to hear the authenticity of your own words…speaking *your* mind. No one ever said, life would be easy, but my experience is that telling the truth ultimately makes everything in life *easier!* To stifle or suppress your voice can (and will) turn into a living nightmare!

Many years ago, Werner Erhard created a course called *"Nature of Reality."* One of the lessons the instructor taught changed my communication skills and life forever. He had us stand in front of a participant, a mirror, or a *very* understanding friend, and speak continuously as if a microphone was hooked up to our brain. To simply say every *word* that came up *without filtering* the thoughts in any way. Not to worry about how it sounds, not to edit, just to simply speak whatever came up. Personally…I think it's probably best if you do it in the mirror first, and get to know and like yourself, before possibly upsetting or risk losing a friend by speaking *so* freely!

Since the tongue can be like a sharp weapon, it's wise to learn the skills of *being appropriate* in our communications and interactions with others. Most of the time, the truth *can* be spoken with honey instead of venom.

I had to learn *not to accuse*, but rather to let people know *how I feel*. I actually had to learn a *new* vocabulary that didn't insult or offend others, but rather one that inspired and empowered others (and to continuously tell the truth at the same time). This new way of communicating also inspired and empowered me. I learned not to be afraid. Fear can create a lot of tension and anxiety! I had to learn to lovingly and gently tell people how I feel *without* making them wrong, *or* dictating to them.

To communicate in this manner is a huge responsibility and accomplishment for anyone! Most of us tend to place blame and point fingers at others, instead of looking within to communicate what we're *really* feeling. I'm still working on this one! My lessons became much easier when I realized that fear and faith cannot live in the same place at the same time. Living in faith is fun, because you have to turn your *ignorance* and arrogance over to a higher power. Admitting that you "don't know" opens up space for you "to know."

Realize at times that the *cost* of your sincere communication with yourself and others can be expensive, but the *payoffs* and *rewards* are almost always priceless, and yet…occasionally, may be painful.

I'm anticipating this book will help ease and lighten the pain, of some of your lessons or even spare you the customary agony or discomfort that life might otherwise bring your way, simply by learning not to *react* or lash out.

If we watch closely, we'll notice what I call the built in *nonsense detector*. As we pay attention, it will keep us on the straight and narrow. It's that same little inner-heart voice I keep speaking about. It always tells us which way to go…right, left, stay home, don't, yes, no. The voice is always there! The more in-tune we become with that voice…ultimately, the freer we become. So many times, I haven't wanted to hear what that inner-voice was saying so I didn't listen and made a different choice to do something another way. But the truth is…*not to listen* just doesn't work. Only when we honor that inner-truth does life become more and more effortless and fun. Growth occurs when you listen to that inner-voice *as opposed to* the antagonistic/rebel dialogue of the mind.

You know, I still have days where I *begin* to feel sad. I still have days when I don't want to get out of bed because it all seems so pointless. Then I remember *gratitude*. When you truly become grateful for what you do have, you can't be sorrowful or sad! I simply look down and see my limbs, and I'm truly grateful. I see the sun shining, the green of the grass and the trees, and I'm so thankful. I have friends who are amazing. I am blessed with a roof over my head and food in my belly. When I don't suppress, *and* I stay in touch with all of that goodness, I just can't be depressed. If you're living as a *victim* or *underdog*, I can tell you now that it does not serve anyone...especially *you!*

Growth comes when you *get in touch* with all that you already have. Then, you can build onto that, any future you choose for yourself. It's really important to *write down* what we are already grateful for. Being thankful for what you *do* have truly keeps everything in perspective because when you *change your thinking* you change your energy patterns which ultimately changes your life!

A few affirmations I say when I'm *grateful* are:

- "I am grateful for living my life in true freedom!"
- "I am grateful for having time to live!"
- "I am grateful for having clarity, choice and true mental balance!"
- "I give thanks for the joys and gifts of life!"
- "I give thanks for my spacious, beautiful, calm and serene home!"

Within reason, there is pretty much nothing that we can't do in life! The *enemy* comes when we listen to the antagonistic rebel voice and the negative comments of others. The drama and turmoil diminish when we give up and live from our truth. That's when life flows effortlessly with joy.

It is my prayer that anyone who reads this book is automatically accelerated to attain the dreams and goals, they desire. That you "do the work" and "go the distance" to reach the heights you aspire to. May you be taken to a new level of well-being in every aspect of your life. And, finally, that you truly take care of the body you were gifted with, for there is a child of beauty in each and every one of us just crying to be honorably released and liberated...without interference!

What visions and dreams have lived and are residing within *your* heart? Are you currently living the life you constructed and contrived for yourself as a young child? Let's take a journey now, and look at *your* higher purpose. Let's find the dreams *you buried away* so long ago.

"You can never get enough of what you really don't want!"

\- Stewart Emery

Finding Your Purpose and Inner Vision!
It lives within you... find it NOW!

Once more I sat alone, awaiting my turn
Growing more nervous by the minute
And doubting the relevance
Of my Quiet Desperation!

- Milton Acorn

Trying to always *force* things into place is exhausting. As previously mentioned, it's very important to have a *written* detailed map of *where* you want to go. It's a good idea to include all your current *dreams, goals,* and *desires,* keeping your focus on your final destination *always* in mind.

See the BIG PICTURE *before* it happens! When I moved into my first home, it was a tiny 2-bedroom tract home. You know the ones, where every house in the neighborhood looks almost identical. I didn't have much money, but I remembered my mom telling me as a young woman, "to make your home into your palace, no matter how bad things appear in your life." When I moved in, there wasn't a blade of grass or a tree in sight.

Throughout the years, as my faith grew, I knew I wanted to live in a tropical paradise, so I planted an assortment of flowers, trees, and bushes throughout my yard. Over time, many things began to blossom and bloom into my very own *Garden of Eden.* Eventually I had a sunroom built to overlook my entire backyard paradise. Each day, as I sit and write, I watch the birds, rabbits, and squirrels merrily frolic just a few feet away from me. They bring joy to my life and comfort to my soul. My modest home has *become* my palace. It is through visualizations, affirmations, taking action, being grateful, and finally...thanking our creator *ahead of time* for answering my prayers...as if my dreams had already been realized.

Without first having beautiful visions, beliefs, and an amazing imagination, including *faith,* I know I would have nothing today. Without a purpose or a goal, we merely survive in fear, living quiet lives of desperation. This usually looks like working a menial job for a minimum wage and doing what you don't enjoy...never giving your self *time* to realize your dreams or doing what you love!

My modest home (which was first conceived in my mind) is now a sanctuary where friends and family can come to just hang out and enjoy life. I've designed each room to be multi-functioning and used for many purposes. My bedroom is not only a place to sleep, but also designed as a sacred space for me to meditate, do yoga, and listen to music. My sunroom is my bright, sunny office, and also has 2 sofa beds to accommodate out of town guests. It's also a great place to read, take naps, or visit with friends.

My living room is the TV room, but is also arranged to accommodate 35 people for meetings, gatherings, and seminars. I gave up a dining room in order to accomplish this. Most things in life are give and take. What are you *willing* to *give up* to attain your goals and live your dreams?

I love my tiny, modest home. I feel so blessed to be able to reside in this happy place for as long as it will continue. It's designed to *inspire me* to hang around, be at peace, and write, which is my current *chosen* profession. When my book is complete, I'll *check in* to see what's next. It's all a mystery to me. I basically *stopped planning* and go with the flow nowadays, even though I do have a general outline and idea of the possibilities. I stopped receiving a typical "traditional paycheck" back in 1989, yet the bills always get paid.

It doesn't matter how long it takes to attain your dreams. What matters is the journey. By listening to our heart and taking action on what we hear, we'll always know the direction to take. We get to experience life on a grand scale just by stopping to smell the roses everyday. A whole world of possibilities opened up for me when I stopped taking things for granted, and learned the true meaning of gratitude and how to pay attention.

Our dreams, goals and desires are merely *visions.* How can we even hope to arrive at a destination without first having a vivid vision of where we want to ultimately be? The visions and dreams are so real for me, that I live most days as if they have *already* come true.

Even when I was very much in debt, I allowed myself to feel wonderful and rich! We can't allow our *circumstances* to dictate or determine our future. What really matters is *what we are telling ourselves*! This is where *affirmations* are so important.

Make great use of every minute. Even if you're just driving to and from work, that's a wonderful time to pop a book on tape or one of Michele Blood's audio cassettes or CD's into the player and sing along. I love her work! Here are a few of her songs from "Be a Magnet to Money."

- o I greet this day with love in my heart.
- o I am living this day, as if it was my last.
- o Today I begin a new life.
- o Today my life has a new start.
- o I greet this day with love in my heart!
- o Today I have a brand new glow, for I am energy.
- o I'm full of life my actions show, that I am energy.
- o I feel alive, now I can see, a brighter future is here for me
- o No one can stop me now!

Always remember…it's perfectly normal to *re-adjust* your dreams, goals and visions along the way. Sometimes we envision or perceive our final destination to *look* a certain way, but in reality, when we finally arrive, it doesn't even appear *close* to what we thought it would look like. This is why it's always important to enjoy the journey, because you're *constructing your reality into existence* as you go.

When I was a young child, I always had the thought that I wanted to be an interior designer. I actually took the necessary steps to reach that goal. I went to the *Maryland Institute School of Art*, but halfway through I realized it didn't fit my pictures (or personality) anymore. I'm thrilled it turned out this way because it helped me figure out that I wanted to design my own homes, *as a hobby*. I found out through actual experience later on, that I didn't enjoy running around to find different fabrics and furniture for other people. It just wasn't my idea of fun.

The talents I developed at the *Institute* however, actually took me in an entirely different direction. Many years later, I started to hand-paint on silk fabric, which led to an extremely lucrative business. I began doing trunk shows at some of the *Nordstrom* locations around the country. Also, the *Smithsonian Institute Gift Shop* commissioned me to paint scenes on silk that related to local events in conjunction with their exhibits. This also eventually became tiresome and boring, which led to my eventual importing of hand-painted silks from China.

I began to wholesale silk products to stores and resorts throughout the United States. This business enabled me to travel to different parts of the world that I might not have otherwise had the opportunity to do. Some of the locations I visited numerous times were China, Hong Kong, Thailand, Hawaii, and all over Europe. My travels also took me to many large cities all across the United States. What I discovered is that everything one does in life inevitably leads to where you are destined to be, especially if you pay attention. Life then becomes a daily *adventure*, rather than a series of burdens. So why not choose to make *your* expedition enjoyable?

Just keep tuned in to that inner-voice and the path will become very obvious…almost as if you were being guided by radar. Also, worlds of new *possibilities* will occur and dreams will become more attainable. There's no telling where in the world you will end up, when you keep listening and continuing to take action. Life will never be dull when you go for your dreams. Getting around in life is surprisingly easy once you stop coming up with *reasons and excuses* why you *can't* do something! *When you give up your excuses, you'll have the results you want!*

Through our intuition, we are always able to create whatever resources are necessary to handle or deal with every situation that arises. I've found that it's true…we are always only 1 or 2 phone calls or contacts away from everything we ever wanted or needed in life!

If something doesn't *feel* right…then it probably isn't! If you get a tremendous "*Yes*" with passion oozing from your heart, and you get joy-bumps of happiness, then for goodness sake, especially your own…just do it! It'll not only benefit you, it will benefit everyone else as well!

I often use a term called "mind-pollution." It's when the little spirit-voice gives you the perfect solution for what to do next, and instead of doing it, the constant gnawing of the antagonistic rebel voice takes over and keeps trying to talk you out of what you *know* is right for you! Tell it to take a hike…"buzz off," thank it for sharing, and then, go live your life! *The mind* can and will play dismal games with you…if you allow it to. Be bigger than your mind, because you *are.*

Don't confuse the voices! Over time you'll learn how to discern the heart/spirit-voice *from* the voice of the antagonistic rebel. Remember to always keep your integrity level high *and* inspire and empower others along the way. All this happens naturally by *being* your authentic self!

Having a *purpose* is important! The translation of purpose *is* aim, determination or expectation.

> *I am always living in* determination
> *That a certain outcome will emerge.*
> *I am always aiming with* intentions
> *That my dreams are not only coming true,*
> *But that they've already arrived,*
> *As if in the 3rd dimension!*
>
> - J'en El

Intentions are *designed plans.* I must have realistic expectations on a daily basis that my plans not only will come to fruition, but that they have *already* come to fruition!

I must know that my day is already joy filled because I'm doing things I want to do, and doing things that make me feel good. I know that when I feel good, I'm able to contribute to the world in extraordinary and soul-satisfying ways.

Some people get confused. They ask, *"How can I make or find the time to do what I want to do, when my life is already so filled with responsibilities to keep up with on a daily basis?"* If you stick with me here, you'll clearly see how the cycle works. In order to *find* the time, you must first *make* the time. You make the time by *nurturing yourself first!* This needs to be done every day! And to do this, you might need to enlist others to aid, support, or assist you in achieving your goals, dreams, or visions. Look at your life to see which people would benefit the most from supporting you. Would it be a spouse, mate, family member, friend, neighbor, co-worker, or a volunteer at a local church?

Ask yourself...

1. How could you *benefit* another person, by having *them* assist *you?*

2. Why would a spouse, neighbor, or anyone want to donate their time to you?

The *answers* vary...

- If your mate or family assisted you in getting more things accomplished, you'd feel more rested and clear-headed which would enable you to spend more *quality,* loving time with them.

- You could be exchanging favors with friends and neighbors, who will in turn help alleviate someone else's full schedule.

Let's say your children attend the same school as your neighbors. You can alternate driving with 5 different people so that you're now driving the children to school only one day a week instead of 5 days per week.

It's okay to ask others for assistance if your life feels too full to cope. Remember, "No man is an island." I get tired if I even think about having to cook, clean, do laundry, shop for groceries, drive to a job, floss, take care of children, and pay bills. Those are exhausting thoughts. We must face the facts and accept that life has been too full (if it has), and get out of the rut. Remember...we're always just one or two phone calls away from having what we want, need, or desire in life! All that's required is to ask for what you want, and then give thanks for having already received it.

- Maybe your boss would allow you to do some of the work from home, or maybe you could work three or four *longer days* and take off the rest of the week.

- *Delegate chores* to your mate and/or family members. This would give them a better sense of accomplishment, and it also frees up your time to do more of what you want.

My experience is that there are always one or more people out there who would be willing and even glad to be of service and assistance to another human being. Sometimes, all it takes is to *ask!* Never be too proud to ask for help! That would be a dis-service to you *and* everyone else!

You might need to get a bit creative...but what price are you willing to pay for your freedom? Right now, unfortunately, most people are *literally paying with their lives!* As mentioned before, personally, that's an intolerable amount to pay. Remember...you are a trainer and personal coach to your children. If they see you as a servant, they will grow up with the same mentality. They'll do what you do! Wouldn't it be better to give them responsibilities at a young age so they are prepared as they grow to be free, capable, and happy?

Children are a huge responsibility and very expensive if they are to get the care they need in today's world. If you already have children, then you need to do everything you can to assist them in getting in touch with the things they love to do, and assist them in having their dreams come true!

If you have *not* had children yet, then you really need to *think* before you do. They need constant loving care, attention, and devotion. They need *you!* We no longer have to take on things bigger than we are! What's the hurry? When you are ready to have a child, then it's a really good idea to bring one into existence. Having one child and learning *their* unique nature makes a lot of sense. You and your mate can be with that child, one on one! Then, if you want to have more, go for it. Remember, we're their custodians! Kahlil Gibran, in his book *"The Prophet,"* writes beautifully about this.

If you know that you need to work a full-time job in order to pay the bills, and have to call on the support of a baby sitter or pre-school, then it's *really* a good idea to wait before bringing another human onto this planet. Most children are simply and tragically *not* having their needs met. Day care facilities are not the most ideal way to bring up a child...but spare yourself of the guilt if you find it necessary! Just keep loving them and yourself!

Taste life and get to know yourself first, then your mate. Build your careers and *then* if you both wish to have a child, raise your child with ease and in a mature and responsible way. Most people *don't* take the time to *think it through first* and are on "automatic" when it comes to bringing children into the world before they're prepared. I notice and think it's great that a lot of couples are *waiting* 'til they're in their late 30s or early 40s to bring children into the world and have a family.

We must be responsible and conscious about our choices in our overpopulated planet. We don't need to add to the insanity. If *we're* not responsible, then everyone loses...you, your child, and everyone in society. We must be an example for our children by living our lives and dreams fully, *in front of them*, which will give them permission to do the same. Too many people stop short of living their dreams once they begin to have they're own family.

So, how do we know which path to take in order to live fully? Remember...your perfect answer always arrives when you are listening and closely paying attention. I believe that messengers or "angels" are sent to us in many forms. Maybe a best friend, a co-worker, a family member, a passer-by, a next-door neighbor, or even the person standing next to you in the grocery line.

These messengers help to get us through challenges in our lives. Hearing the truth may be painful at times, yet it's *essential!* What makes it easier is if we are willing to hear the truth, then we start finding it to be exciting and actually look forward to change. When we learn to discern the truth from jealousy and manipulation, we spare ourselves from enduring long-term pain, both in the present as well as in the future. True friends will tell us what they see, so we can have long-term gains. That's what a friend is for. To assist with our quick, long-term growth, inevitably guiding us to a better life. If you listen closely, your inner spirit/heart-voice is your truest friend. When you listen to that, you'll reach *Nirvana,* which is heaven on earth.

Sometimes in the process of attaining *Nirvana* we will come across obstacles appearing in many different forms. One of the most unrecognizable one is *manipulation.* When someone wishes to manipulate you or exploit you, they misrepresent their intentions with crafty deception. This is fraud at it's finest. In fact, it's a form of rape! Because it's so covert, we don't even see it coming our way a lot of the time...until it's too late. Sometimes the perpetrator isn't even aware they are scheming to create a specific outcome. I see manipulation/exploitation as cheating and dishonest, and completely lacking empathy, compassion, and understanding.

The source of manipulation is mistrust, fear, or *lack.* When someone does not feel cared about by the universe or their creator, again, they manipulate and exploit in order to create a specific experience. If we could keep in mind that we've always been (and are) an essential expression of, and *never separate from,* our divine creator, then fear of loss or becoming separate from *that which lovingly brought us into existence would never arise!* The moment *our betrayers (or we)* give up manipulation and deception...is the very moment that the feeling of separateness dissolves. This of course leads to the discovery of *who* we really are, and to finding our true selves, and our essential nature. The challenges with deception and manipulation are that sometimes we just don't recognize we've been deceived until it's late in the game. We don't need to become paranoid about *who's trying to get us,* we simply need to stay awake and not deceive ourselves.

By paying attention to our true needs, wants, and desires, we will "*stop putting our life on hold!*" It's okay to listen now to what your inner-voice is screaming for. Paying attention to the words and taking action will give birth to immense joy in your life. It's okay to start enjoying life this very second! Consider yourself already where you wish to be...a done deal! If that's so, then there's nothing else to do except just *be* and have fun. Begin filling your daily schedule with things that enrich you, rather than exhaust you.

Ask yourself:

> What are you doing to create happiness?
> What would fill you with joy?

Go ahead...give yourself *"permission"* to *go for it* and *have it all!* Remember that everything you do matters! Never discount your actions, because the choices you make...good *or* bad, ultimately affect everyone! Think before you speak. Blending kindness with truth works best.

Remember to B R E A T H E!

You will continue to find specific formulas throughout the chapters, which will explain in detail exact methods and ways to feel whole, complete, invigorated, energized, and healthy a majority of the time. We need to *do the work* to feel comfort in our own skin!

Not knowing your *purpose* would be like walking in circles through the dessert aimlessly. To me, that equates to pain and/or death of your soul...and even downright stupidity!

How do you find your purpose?

Get out a sheet of paper *now* and write down all of the things from your earliest memories that made you feel good, whole, energized, complete, loved, and lovable.

It doesn't matter what anyone else thinks. Write down the things that *really* turn you on. What puts a smile on your face? It's different for everyone. It could be looking at the stars. It could be walking on the beach. It could be water skiing. It could be stamp collecting. It could be talking on the phone, writing poetry, or buying shoes. It's no one's business but yours.

Don't ever let anyone dictate or tell you what makes you feel good *or* tell you what's *right* for you! As a matter of fact, never let anyone intimidate you *ever* again! If someone tries to intimidate you, it simply means that they are trying to *make you wrong* or to bully you because *they* feel inadequate! Never give your power to anyone. Your heart and soul and spirit are yours. It's the universe's way of making you be the unique and beautiful person that lives inside of that magnificent body of yours.

Sometimes life reminds me of a baseball game in perpetual motion. I always know where first base it located. I put together a plan and strategy about how to get there, always stopping to smell the roses along the way, and being grateful for what I have. Then, I glide *ever so gently* toward the next base. I've had to learn to *be gentle* with myself and *give myself a break*...especially when I occasionally get off course. It's not nice to beat anyone up for getting off track, especially our "selves." We wouldn't be angry with anyone else for *tripping* along the way, so why would we be insensitive with the very person living in our own skin?

If you attain a goal and realize it's absolutely *not* what makes you happy from every possible angle, then acknowledge that and continue checking in and self-correcting and readjusting your goals along the way. There could be various reasons why something didn't turn out to be *or* feel right for you, but it doesn't matter *why.* Maybe it wasn't the way you had imagined it would be. Or, you may not have *thoroughly thought a plan through.*

Maybe the final destination wasn't quite what you thought it would be. Whatever the case, this is the perfect time to check in with yourself and *forgive yourself* and others if necessary for miscalculating along the way, and/or wasting precious time, and *move on!* Turn the lemon into lemon-aid!

If we're fortunate, we realize everything we do is *never* a waste of time or mistake, but rather a learning experience which takes us onward and upward, gradually proceeding toward our next dream, goal, or vision enjoyably toward the next base. But don't forget to remind yourself that you're "always already at home base" during the entire journey!

Most people unfortunately believe they're *stuck* with what they've got. That's Nonsense! It's okay to change course. Be sure to *acknowledge* your new truth or goal, *everyday* if necessary. What looks like *errors* along the way will all fit into place sooner or later! Sometimes years may pass before you understand why you took that *original* path. It will all add up to a peaceful existence if you keep listening, learning, and acting on your dreams. After all, life is a buffet.

Almost everything looks good. Until you taste it, how could you possibly know in advance what you like or don't? That's why there are 31+ flavors, and even though there are, I still like vanilla the best. And, it's also okay to like more than one thing at a time. It's perfectly fine and natural to be an airline pilot, *and* an architect, *and* a musician, *and* a chef! My brother can play 5 instruments and thoroughly enjoys it. However, he decided to become an anesthesiologist as his main profession.

The journey of self-discovery is fun once we allow it to be. So what, if it takes weeks, months, years, or a lifetime to get it right? I think one of the keys is to keep being loving and gentle and kind to you and everyone else along the way. We all really deserve *everything* that we desire!

Most unhappiness appears in our lives when we try to coerce ourselves into some *category.* Just remember to always give yourself a break and be forgiving of your humanness. I used to have a friend who taught me to always listen for the big "YES" before committing to anything or anyone.

"Pushing the River" is trying to force something into existence... going against the grain! I used to do it all the time. It's much better (and easier) to go with the flow by no longer doing the things we don't intrinsically enjoy! It supports no one by being untrue to ourselves! If you've already gotten involved in a situation that doesn't work for you, then find a helpful, winning solution and remove yourself from things that don't feel right and move forward before you sink in deeper!

The following story came via email. It's one of my favorites. It sums things up nicely. Enjoy!

A Thousand Marbles

"Well, Tom, it sounds like you're too busy with your job to even see your children grow up and enjoy your life. Such a young fellow, and having to work 70 hours per week. I'm sure they must pay you well, but it's a shame you have to be away from home and your family so much.

He continued, "Let me tell you something that has helped me keep a good perspective on my own priorities."

"You see, I sat down one day and did a little arithmetic. The *average* person lives about 75 years. "So, I multiplied 75 times 52 and I came up with 3,900 which is the number of Saturdays that the average person has in their entire lifetime.

"It took me until I was 55 years old to think about all this in much detail," he went on, "and by that time, I had already lived through over 2800 Saturdays. I got to thinking that if I only lived to be 75, I only had about a thousand of them left to enjoy. "So I went to a toy store and bought every single marble they had. I ended up having to visit three toy stores to round up 1,000 marbles. I took them home and put them inside of a large, clear plastic container, right here on my desk, where I sit on a daily basis.

Every Saturday since then, I have taken one marble out and thrown it away. "I found that by watching the marbles diminish, I focused more on the really important things in life; the things that matter to me; the things that put a smile on my face. There is nothing like watching your time here on this earth run out, to help get your priorities straight."

"Now let me tell you one last thing before I sign-off with you and take my lovely wife out for breakfast. This morning, I took the very last marble out of the container. I figure if I make it until next Saturday, then I have been given a little extra time here on this planet. One thing we can all use is a little more time."

"It was nice to meet you Tom, I hope you spend more time with your family, and doing the things you LOVE to do! And, I hope to meet you again." You could have heard a pin drop on the radio when this fellow signed off.

I guess he gave us all a lot to think about. I had planned to work that morning. Instead, I went upstairs and woke my wife up with a kiss. "C'mon honey, I'm taking you and the kids to breakfast."

..."What brought this on?" she asked with a smile. Oh, nothing special, it's just been a while since we spent a Saturday together with the kids. Hey, can we stop at a toy store while we're out? I need to buy some marbles."

MAY ALL OF YOUR SATURDAYS BE SPECIAL!

-Unknown

Design Your Most Perfect World.
Differentiate the heart-voice from a hostile takeover!

Our *actions* speak VOLUMES! We can say anything…but it's what we do that *really* matters in life. Doing what we say makes us accountable. Being accountable is both wise and responsible. Since our word is all we really have in life, we must be careful for what we say and promise to others. People count on us to do what we say! When we don't keep our word, we create a mess and leave a trail of destruction and casualties behind us. It's simply hurtful and damaging to say we'll do something, and then NOT do it.

The way to avoid this is to think things through *before* you make promises. If you really can't keep your word, then clean up the dilemma with whomever you made the promise to. Check in to see what kind of trail you've been leaving in the world? Are you making a positive difference in the lives of people you touch?

To give someone the silent treatment is a sure way to kill off the relationship. Communication is not only necessary; it's indispensable, essential, and even critical. Honest communication, along with action is so vital, because it penetrates and pierces the soul of people we know, love, and *supposedly* care about. *Not* to communicate is to abandon and neglect those very people we say we're in love with. Life can be a win-win for us all when we speak from our hearts without blame.

There is never anything to fear when you speak your truth. After each communication, it is vital, however, for you to be there as a *safe space* for the other person, so that they can process your words and speak *their truth* back to you. Wars would cease when people finally figure out that life is *not* about me *or* you; but rather me *and* you. There's enough of everything to go around...especially LOVE! There are simply No Shortages! We must learn how to communicate our truth!

Have you ever walked away from a person and heard them *mumble under they're breath?* I hate that! My partner used to do it fairly often. Finally, I confronted him simply by saying... *"What did you say?"* After his reply of... *"nothing,"* I gently let him know *"how sad it made me feel"* that he didn't feel safe enough to communicate to me directly and honestly. I also let him know if he continued to suppress his anger by mumbling to himself, we could never resolve any difference of opinions that existed. I also told him that if he continued doing this that one day he would have a "stack attack,"

Having a stack attack is when someone unleashes all the built up stress and anger they have been suppressing...usually with blame and accusation. How can you ever get to the bottom of something when it's covered over with lies and hurt feelings? What a mess! Wouldn't it be easier to simply *speak your truth as it happens* and then move on with your life running smoothly, like a fine-tuned machine? Of course you must be prepared to truly listen to and hear what the other person has to say without judging or invalidating. Just listen!

We must first communicate honestly with ourselves. In our society, most of us were taught at a very young age that it was selfish to put yourself first in any way, shape, or form. My beliefs are just the opposite! I conclude that it's best, and even great, to put yourself first, as long as you're not wounding others along the way.

If your doctor told you that you only had a limited amount of time to live, what would you do? I bet you'd fulfill *all* of the things you ever dreamt about. You'd find a way to make your dreams come true without postponing your life any longer. I know most people would not only live their life differently, but also *see* their life differently.

After the initial shock of finding out you were going to die (sooner than later), your new perspective would probably be...I better start living my passion and dreams out loud...right *now!* You'd know immediately what your *time* is *really* worth! And, there would be no doubts about the things that turn you on and make you happiest in the world.

Since we're all ultimately and inevitably going to die anyway, why not give up the option right now of postponing what we really want to do, and start living today as if it really is our last. I bet you'd just fall in love with yourself over and over again, just by being good to yourself, and living your dreams. The more I began to give and do for myself, the more accepting I became of who I am, and the better and more enjoyable, life became, and the more good I see in others. Ultimately, I'm less selfish because I'm so well taken care of that I can now be there for others.

In learning to change my thoughts, I was then able to *allow myself to just be.* I no longer had to *tolerate* who I thought I was, but I was able to *be at ease* and love the person who I decided to become. When you do enough work on yourself, one day, you just wake up and like the person you see in the reflection. You can't help but feel comfortable in your own skin. That makes everyday beautiful!

Most of us don't make or take the time or *allow* ourselves to nurture and pamper that little god or goddess within. We don't need to wait until we're 30, 40, 50, or even 60 to be fabulous! That just wastes the precious time we have left on this planet. There are only a few reasons a person would wait to have life be wonderful. Let's start with *fear.* Fear leads to insecurity. *Insecurity* leads to vulnerability. *Vulnerability* leads to exposure. Since exposure means to disclose, it makes one wonder..."What are we afraid of disclosing?" It all leads back to **fear**!

What exactly are we afraid of?

> ➤ *Who* I am?
> ➤ What I *want?*
> ➤ *Getting* what I want?

<u>My questions became...</u>

- What changes *am I* we *willing* to make...in order to attain what I want?
- How *lazy* am I?
- Why do I make *others* more important than I am?
- Why would I make *anyone* more important than I am?

Maybe it's because we think we have *forever* to align with *our* personal passion. Life is far *too short* to be wasting precious time! Sometimes, finding our *passion* takes research. Research within. As the years passed by, the more frantically, I searched for answers... *"Please God, show me who I am and why I'm here. Let me make a difference during my stay here on this planet. What are the personal contributions I am to make?"*

In the search to find my legacy, I was reminded by my mom about the contributions I *naturally* made as a young child. She said I always brought in *strays*, but not necessarily stray animals. In my case, it was usually more *"human strays."* "Stray" is simply someone who deviates from his or her chosen path. Every once in a while I see myself as a mechanic or tow truck driver. Someone looks *lost* on the path of life, and I just aid in jumpstarting their engine. That's been my gift. To assist people in re-aligning with their dreams and goals when they get off track. Then they move on, back into the world, making a difference again, and contributing to others.

The movie *"Pay it Forward"* is the perfect example of showing how one good turn is passed on to another. I'm a true believer in *"What goes around... comes around."* Life ultimately begins to look like a flawless chain of events when you align with your passion *and* find your legacy. Fear naturally dissolves as you go out and make *your* difference in the world. Of course occasionally plenty of trial and error occurs in finding the accurate *vehicle* or *platform* to use when making a difference on a grand scale. But, I've found that there are numerous ways to touch the masses! So, let's begin by being in touch with, fine tuning, adjusting, and improving *ourselves!*

How much will it all matter in the scheme of things? Who are we trying to fix? Someone once asked Mother Theresa how she was

67

able to assist so many people. Her reply was... *"I helped one person at a time!"* This makes *anything* possible for you and me!

There are so many people who touch our lives and leave imprints in our hearts and touch our souls. Oprah touches the lives of millions on a daily basis. In today's world, there are various ways to impact and instill the world with our ideas. Television, books, magazines, CDs, DVDs, audiocassettes, videocassettes, records, web sites, email, and the list goes on! Mariah, Celine, and Barbra touch so many lives with their songs. My dear friend, Dr. Edith Eva Eger, who survived the Holocaust, continues to teach the message of forgiveness and appreciation in her lectures. Dr. Terry Cole-Whittaker shares her spiritual zest for life. Dr. Martin Luther King inspired the world with his dreams, visions, and oratory skills. Maya Angelo inspires with her poetry and spirit. Mattie J.T. Stepanek touches people with his loving, understanding heart, and role as Peacemaker. Michele Blood with her Affirmations in Song, her caring heart, and illuminating energy. Dr. Phil touches us with his no nonsense insight, knowledge, and humor. Using the *Course in Miracles*, Marianne Williamson teaches people to love and relax. Helen Gurley Brown, Caroline Myss...and the list goes on.

There are so many others that it would fill an encyclopedia. Thank you all so very much for your work. You have breathed life and genuine hope into millions of people worldwide!

My question became... *"How was I, supposed to touch the hearts and souls of humanity? How could I make a difference and be of any significance on this immense planet?"* I prayed for guidance and then one day as I looked into the mirror while naked, my life changed forever! I was to finally *know* what it feels like...to find comfort in my own skin.

The Real You!
...Look in the Mirror Naked and Find Out "Who" You Really Are!

"I learned this at least from my experience...
If you advance confidently in the direction of your dreams,
And endeavor to live the life you have imagined,
You will meet with a success unexpected in common hours.
You will pass an invisible boundary.
New universal and more liberal laws will begin to
Establish themselves around and within you,
And you will live with the license of a higher order of beings.
If you have built castles in the air, your work need not be lost
That is where they should be.
Now...put the foundation under them."

- Henry David Thoreau

It's perfectly natural for us all to enjoy *both sides* of our brain. The *right side* of the brain is my favorite! It's where imagination is expressed, and where creative juices are allowed to frolic freely without care. To "walk on the wild side" and tap into our artistic and poetic freedom. Our right brain is where independence and autonomy reign. It's where we access our mystical self. It's sometimes referred to as "the female side." but men possess it as well. It's the side most of us have been taught to suppress from an early age. We're taught to grow up and be exactly like the authority figures who raised us in "their image" instead of teaching us to search within ourselves to find our own individual, unique, artistic, and poetic creativity which are major parts of our identity.

The *left side* of our brain is known as the more masculine, analytical, and logical side. It's the corporate-thinking mentality that enables us to do enterprising and successful business deals. Both sides of our brain are equally important so that we can live compatibly in harmony and happiness within ourselves, as well as co-exist peacefully in the world. Men and woman never need to compete. Our differing points of views are required in order to live a balanced life, but hopefully *without* conflict, hostility, and wars!

When you *come home to yourself* and love *who* and *what* you are, you'll know you have arrived at heaven on earth!

The older I become, the more feminine and at peace I feel. I've learned over time to be glad I'm a woman, but this wasn't always the case. I used to think that because males dominated they had it easier than females.

Women actually got more than they ever bargained for when it came to fighting for *equal rights*. We burned our bras and demanded our voices be heard. I found that most people actually don't need to be *right*, more importantly we have a need to *be heard* without being made wrong for having certain thoughts. Let's face it, there are two sides to every coin, and there are usually at least two different points of views about everything in life. Can you imagine how boring living would be if everyone thought and acted identically?

It's back to the "pendulum theory" again. It's all about finding *center* and *balance*, as well as feeling comfortable in your own skin. It's about looking in the mirror and liking "who" we see. Knowing we're the very best we can be. Getting to know that little inner child who resides in our heart. That inner child who *always* knew *everything* was possible!

Learn to *embrace* and cherish your inner-child. See it as your personal built-in *light worker and protector* who lovingly sits on the sidelines, watching, feeling, and guiding everything that goes on in your life. Treat your inner-child as a special soothing presence sent by God, for it will always let you know through an innocent heart, what is *right* for you at every moment…when you are "in tune."

I guess the best way to describe the communication a person has with their inner child is by way of *feelings or telepathy*. Recently, my inner-child and I began to communicate after many years of silent neglect. I *envision "us"…my inner-child and I,* sitting on a dock, hand in hand, laughing and talking about what puts a smile on our faces, and what brings joy to our hearts.

As a result, "we've" learned a technique to *release people from our lives* who have been harmful to "us" in any way. The method used to do this is to perceive people, who have deceived or betrayed us as floating off in a hot air balloon, until they disappear. We laugh and wave goodbye to them, as we *thank them* for the contributions they've made to our lives, and *forgive them* for being mean-spirited to us. We wish them no harm, and we wish them well, but above all, we pray that if at all possible…they *never* cross our paths again unless and until they are there to make a life-positive contribution!

It's said that a great way to protect ourselves is with imaginary white light, as well as pyramid shaped mirrors, which insulates and shields us from any negative forces that try to penetrate our inner-sanctum of peace and harmony. The bright light shines from above. It goes in through our head *chakra* beaming downward through every cell of our body until we feel firmly embedded to the core of nature. Talk about *feeling at one with the universe!* With this kind of belief system and grounding in place, how can anything unfavorable happen to anyone? If any mean-spirited people show up, they couldn't possibly penetrate our light, no matter how hard they try.

I realize how unusual this may sound to some people, but it really works! I used to be so empathic, that I would take on everyone's emotions and stories. It was actually so physically painful I would walk around in a fog of depression. I made a vow to *never let that happen again.* People's energies vary. We must learn to surround ourselves with caring, loving human beings who are always aligned with our higher good. They're called light workers, and they're interspersed among us everywhere on the planet. They're just people like you and me, however, their consciousness is more illumined and loving. They are awake and aware!

If you feel in any way desperate for guidance, it's important to hear what your inner/heart-voice is revealing. Before I began writing this book I remember crying uncontrollably. As the tears flowed down my cheeks, I harshly screamed out to the *imposter* who showed up in my reflection… *"Who are you and what do you want with me?"* The tears that burst forth from "me" *and* "my image in the mirror" turned into tears of joy as the answers became clear. The fraud that had previously appeared, vanished into thin air as I began to write from my heart, all of the truths that I'd been withholding for so long. The words flowed from the depths of my soul. The paragraphs and pages filled as the hours, days, weeks, and even months flowed, until it became a book...this book!

After 50 years of searching, the obvious became clear! *Distinct possibilities* that had never occurred to me before became apparent and visible in *words*. I found my passion, freedom, and love through expression and communication in writing. I've since found out by watching "Oprah" that I am not alone. That people who have lost their way find comfort and also often become liberated by writing down their deepest thoughts and feelings. A year has passed, and the words and feelings continue to flow. My life has progressed to a new level, as my lessons are being learned at an accelerated pace.

One of my greatest lessons is that there is freedom in doing what you love! Freedom is doing what you love! When you follow and listen to that inner-voice, you'll *always* make a positive difference in people's lives, especially and foremost...your own! If I had paid attention at an earlier age, maybe I would have learned this sooner and not wasted so much precious time. And that is the whole point of this book...to pay attention, find your passion, feel comfort in your own skin, and run with this new zest for life. The new emerged you will be elated and unstoppable!

God gave us each a Palace to reside in. We call it a body, and unfortunately, what we usually do with it is very *destructive*. We test it out like a rented car to see how much abuse it can take. We unconsciously mistreat and abuse it in so many ways and then when it breaks down we hope and think we can turn it in for something new...only to find out that many times, it's simply too late, we've gone too far!

So, we must change our way of thinking and our habits instantly...today! We no longer need to flounder around unconsciously struggling for the answers. For our peace lives in asking the right questions!

<u>We can ask ourselves...</u>

- "What can I do "*right*" today for my body?"
- "What *gift* can I give to myself today?"
- "What is my body *telling me* right now?"

72

<u>The Question really is</u>...

... *"What* is your body *begging for* right now?"

- Healthy food	- Rest	- Water
- Oxygen	- Comfort	- Moisture
- Meditation	- Love	- Nurturing
- Yoga	- Healing	- Laughter
		...The list goes on.

If you look in the mirror *naked* long enough, you'll know exactly what to do for your body. *Confronting your image in this way* will bring up everything from...fear to hatred, to laughter, to tears of joy, to sadness, to pain, to happiness, to upset, to love. If you really want to get serious about *"who"* you are, go to a special, quiet place in your home right now, where you can have privacy and remove your clothing. Take a good long look, and start to consciously BREATHE.

Do it often, because each time, you will see something different. Always REMEMBER...you are so much more than your body! You are a powerful spirit having a physical experience.

<u>As you look at yourself naked, be sure to *affirm*....</u>

- "I appreciate my body, but I am more than my body...I am a Powerful Spirit!"
- "I love and accept myself and eat only the foods that are good for me."
- "I am energy, I exercise regularly."
- "My body is healthy and full of life."

Like a diamond we, as humans, have *facets* and *flaws.* No two are alike, yet all very precious. On what might have been an otherwise *good day,* you might get real depressed when you see that unused, unexercised, unloved body in the reflection. On the other hand, you might have been having a disastrous day, and when you look in the mirror naked, you might become extremely thankful for the simplest things, such as having all of your limbs intact, or a beautiful, inviting, smile. Go ahead...take a look. Be gentle in your "seeing." Please don't hold it against me, if you don't like what's in the reflection. As a matter of fact, don't hold it against anyone...especially yourself!

73

Just remain aware; take responsibility for what you see; and move on. It's never too late to be good to yourself. Be honest with yourself, without being cruel or harsh in the process. We tend to be our own worst enemy at times. Be gentle and loving and caring and *thankful* for what you do have. *Gratitude* is MOST IMPORTANT!

If you think you're too fat, then *"love that fat away."* Breathe into the excess fat (with feeling), until you see muscle resurface (which may take weeks, months, or even longer depending on how much we've let ourselves go). What truly matters is that you start *now* to take care of the body you were blessed with. Remember…it is your *only* palace! Take care of it *now* before it's too late. So be sure you read the chapters on exercise and nutrition many times over! **Do the work!** Remember there's a *cost* for *everything* we do in life, so keep your eye on that that is priceless and honor it!

I don't believe the damage we've done is *ever* irreversible. Isolate each individual area of your body you wish to work on in any particular day. Remember that it literally took you months, years, or even a lifetime to put on that weight and become the way you are at this very moment, so don't expect to see the "physical" miracles occur instantaneously. Simply continue striving each day to get closer to where you want to be. Most assuredly you will *see* and *feel* the difference and get the *results* you want!

It's a joyous moment when your diligence pays off. Be patient with yourself, yet keenly aware of and appreciative for every daily gradual win and accomplishment simply because you've believed; you've kept your faith; and you've prevailed for no other reason than "You're Worth It!" (I'll talk more about this in the chapter on "Breathing, Exercise and Nutrition.").

It's a beautiful moment when you find comfort in your own skin. Do this by taking charge of your body, and gradually mold it to do what it was designed to do. Lovingly declare yourself back into shape; but all with gentle, intelligent, loving care and nurturance. It can be done and it will be done, as soon as you *write that into your script!* Throughout this book you will be given affirmations and information necessary to triumph over your adversities.

One of my dear friends, Dr. Howard Peiper, wrote a book with his partner, Nina Anderson, called *"The Secrets of Staying Young."* It's chock full of essential information about the human body, and speaks of natural ways to turn back the clock. It's extremely well written and easy to read. If you want to understand how foods work in the human body, order their book immediately by calling 1-888-NATURE 1...It's a *must* read!

I heard many years ago that we *do* "write our own script" in life. If that is true, then why on earth would we ever say anything to ourselves other than what's positive?

If in fact, "our words *do* write our world," then why not *design our lives* in a positive way. Stop...with the "I'm so fat" already...or "I'm too ugly, or, "wrinkled and old." Let's face it...it's a fact of life that the body is getting older, but that's no excuse to give up or stop taking care of ourselves...so we need to stop arguing for our conditions and limitations. Doing so, actually hastens the withering away and disease process.

Most of us are living like we have one foot in the grave. I'm talking about looking at your self-naked...really looking "face to face." Asking yourself... *"Who is that person?"* *"Is he or she worth my time?"* *"If NOT...why not?"* *Maintenance* takes time, knowledge, and understanding. If we let our body down, it will surely let us down, and maybe much sooner than we thought in ways we hadn't imagined.

Don't let anyone or anything destroy or hinder your vision...or keep you from attaining your dreams and goals. Your life may not be flawless, but you can take your first tiny step today to make an impact that will change your future. Don't *ever* give anyone the power to penetrate your armor of protection against sabotage and destruction. Always remember to *check in* with yourself when you're feeling hurt or uncomfortable. Don't ever give anyone the ability to make you feel bad! Just don't allow it! Your life is too precious!

I just received the following email from my special friend Ca'Brina. I think this is the perfect place and time to share it. **This is absolutely precious...Enjoy!**

"A Letter from God/Goddess…To Our Children of Earth"

Dear Children…(and believe us… that's all of you)!

We consider ourselves pretty patient folk. For instance, look at the Grand Canyon. It took millions of years to get it right; and, evolution? Boy, nothing is slower than designing that whole Darwinian thing to take place, cell by cell, gene by gene.

We've been patient through your fashions, civilizations, wars and schemes, and the countless ways you take Us for granted until you get yourselves into big trouble again and again.

We want to let you know about some of the things that are starting to tick us off…

First of all, your religious rivalries are driving us up a wall. Enough already! Let's get one thing straight: These are YOUR religions, not Ours! We are the whole enchilada; we're beyond them all! Every one of your religions claims there is only one of Us (which is absolutely true)… But in the very next breath, each religion claims it's "Our" favorite one. And, each claims its scriptures were written personally by us, and that all the other scriptures are man-made. Oy Vey! How do we even begin to put a stop to such complicated nonsense?

Okay, listen up now. We're your Father and Mother, and we don't play favorites among our children!

Also, We hate to break it to you, but we don't write! (We did make an exception in this case, even though our longhand is awful). We've always been more of "doers" anyway. Men and women wrote ALL of your books, (including those Bibles). Remarkable people did inspire them, but they also made mistakes here and there. We made sure of that so that you would never trust a written word more than your own living heart!

You see one human being to us…even a bum on the street is worth more than all the Holy Books in the world. That's just the kind of folk we are.

Our spirit is not a "historical thing." It's alive, right here, right now, as fresh as your next breath. Holy books and religious rites are sacred and powerful, but not more so than the least of you. They were only meant to steer you in the right direction, not to keep you arguing with each other, and certainly not to keep you from trusting your own personal connection with Us, which brings us to Our next point about your nonsense. You act like we need you and your religions to stick up for us, or "win souls" for our sake. Please, don't do us any favors! We can stand quite well on our own, thank you! We don't need you to defend us, and we don't need constant credit. We just want you to be good to each other!

And another thing, We don't get all worked up over money or politics, so stop dragging our names into your dramas! For example... We never threatened Oral Roberts. We never rode in any of Rajneesh's Rolls-Royces. We never told Pat Robertson to run for president, and we've never, EVER, had a conversation with Jim Baker, Jerry Falwell, or Jimmy Swaggart! Of course, come Judgment Day, We certainly intend to!

The thing is, We want you to stop thinking of religion as some sort of loyalty pledge to us. The true purpose of your religions is so that YOU can become more aware of us, not the other way around. Believe Us, We know you already. We know what's in each of your hearts, and We love you with no strings attached!

Lighten up and enjoy us. That's what religion is best for! What you seem to forget is how mysterious we are. You look at the petty differences in your Scriptures and say, "Well, if THIS is the truth, then THAT can't be!" But instead of trying to figure out Our Paradoxes and Unfathomable Nature; which by the way, you NEVER will, so why not open your hearts to the simple common threads in all religions... You know what We're talking about!

- Love and respect everyone!
- Be kind, even when life is scary or confusing!
- Take courage and be of good cheer... for We are always with you!
- Learn how to be quiet, so you can hear our still, small voice. (We don't like to shout)!

- Leave the world a better place by living your life with dignity and gracefulness, for you are Our Own Children.
- Hold back nothing from life, for the parts of you that can die surely will, and the parts that can't, won't... So don't worry, be happy! (We borrowed that last line from Bobby McFerrin.)

Simple stuff! So why do you keep making it so complicated? It's like you're always looking for an excuse to be upset. And we're very tired of being your main excuse. Do you think we care whether you call us... "Yahweh, Jehovah, Allah, Diana, Brahma, Father, Mother, God, Goddess or even the Void of Nirvana? Do you think we care which of our special children you feel closest to, Jesus, Mary, Buddha, Krishna, Gerald, Mohammed or any of the others? You can call our Special Ones and us any name you choose, if only you would go about Our business of loving one another as We love you. How can you keep neglecting something so simple?

We're not telling you to abandon your religions. Enjoy your religions, honor them, and learn from them, just as you should enjoy, honor, and learn from your parents. But do you walk around telling everyone that your parents are better than theirs are? Your religion, like your parents, may always have the most special place in your hearts. We don't mind that at all. And we don't want you to combine all the Great Traditions in One Big Mess. Each religion is unique for a reason. Each has a unique style so that people can find the best path for themselves. Know that Our Special Children, the ones that your religions revolve around, all live in the same place...(Our heart), and we assure you, they get along perfectly!

The clergy must stop creating a myth of sibling rivalry where there is none. Our blessed children of Earth, the world has grown too small for your pervasive religious bigotry and confusion. Air travel, satellite dishes, telephones, fax machines, rock concerts, diseases, mutual needs and concerns connect the whole planet.

Get with the program! If you really want to help, then commit yourselves to figuring out how to feed your hungry, clothe your naked, protect your abused, and shelter your poor. And just as importantly, make your own everyday life a shining example of kindness and good humor. We've given you all the resources you need, if only you abandon your fear of each other and begin living, loving and laughing together.

We're not really ticked off. We just wanted to grab your attention because we hate to see you suffer. But we have given you free will to choose your own paths, and we just want you to be happy.

In Perfect Love and Perfect Trust, Us.

- Unknown

It's Now Time to Heal and Cleanse
...Make the Transition from Struggle to Renewed ENERGY!

We have a choice about the people we allow into our lives.
We have a choice about the people we elect into office.
We have a choice about our religious beliefs.
We have a choice about being happy and filled with joy
... Rather than being a victim.
We have a choice about the energy level we maintain.
We have a choice about living life in health,
Harmony, peace, and authenticity.
We are not our bills,
And thank goodness...
We are more than our body!

-J'en El

I began writing this chapter because for some ridiculous reason I noticed that I started feeling meek, submissive and even easily manipulated by others. This enabled people with meddling personalities to intrude on my well-being. The last time I remember something like this happening was when I was young and extremely ignorant about life.

It seemed that every time I began to really feel great about something, I noticed that after telling a few people about my dreams, visions and goals, that I began to feel zapped of energy! Literally drained of everything good and powerful that I lived for and believed in. I think *vulnerability* was being confused with *feeble-mindedness*. What was going on?

I began to feel betrayed and deceived by a few people who I cared so deeply about! How could this happen? What was this about? Apparently I had become totally blinded by my naiveté. Because I cared so very much for these "so-called" friends, I just found it hard to believe that they would throw daggers, or malign me in any way. Some of their comments got back to me, and I allowed myself to get so depressed from what I heard, that I would be thoroughly

80

devastated for days and weeks on end. My sadness brought so many tears as a result of feeling violated unjustly.

I was soon to find out that there is a form of manipulation and deception that has been taking place since the beginning of time. It's so powerful, that it actually sucks the life force and energy right out of a human being, without them even being aware of or understanding what is happening.

I had no idea friends, spouses, family members, or even enemies could be so cruel, impolite, discourteous, contemptuous, destructive, jealous, or downright rude, as to wish for another's demise, but boy did I have a lot to learn. Regardless of whether their behavior is conscious or not, doesn't matter; what does matter, is that you recognize the truth, allow it to be so, and *not make excuses* because of your hope, optimism, or original obscured vision about these so called *friends.* Of course if you can communicate your feelings with the person who betrayed you, that's ideal, but, if not…you gotta' move on, 'cause your life and well being depends on it!

Since I know we need to take responsibility for *everything* that occurs in our lives, I really needed to do a lot of soul-searching to figure out what was happening. I hadn't felt or experienced that much pain, since the death of my three closest relatives.

I quickly realized that in order to live out one's passion with energy and vitality, we *must* know where the drains or energy leaks take place, and put a stop to that kind of nonsense immediately! If it weren't for a few of my closest friends, whom I've trusted for years, I really don't think I would have made it through this painful experience. It actually felt like I was sliding into a dark abyss, with nowhere to go but down.

Whether we choose to believe it or not, we need to know that some people have a vested interest in actually seeing us fail, (or *not* grow and succeed). Sometimes, they don't even consciously realize they're impairing our growth or holding us back. Unfortunately, sometimes there's even more of a payoff for people to keep us where we are, than to see us grow and prosper. You might not even recognize the signs until it's too late. Some people automatically assume that if you win…they lose! This is very unfortunate, since there is no shortage of *anything* on our planet. An example would be to look at the latest scandals with *World.com* and *Enron.* We put our trust and faith into authority figures and gave up all responsibility, as if they'd take care of us. We need to learn to take responsibility for our own well-being, as well as to diversify and expand our lives. People usually think in terms of money when they hear the word *diversify.* But I'm talking about opening up all areas of our lives. Seeing the world in new ways, other than what we learned from our closest circles of influence.

Have you noticed that some of the biggest *vampires of your energy* are the very people you trust to let into your home? Your friends, roommates, or spouse can be the biggest drain on your energy. No one has the right to turn you into his or her doormat, dumping ground, or punching bag. Going within and taking a good, long, honest look at yourself, and taking the necessary actions to remedy, correct, repair or change your situation will ultimately lead you to the life you'll enjoy living.

We need to honestly deal with our issues of co-dependency, and determine why we allow certain people into our lives. Did you ever notice that when you meet a potential mate, that the very things you love about them at the beginning of your relationship are the same thing you end up hating about them later on. We always know what's right for us when we really listen and observe. Begin trusting and honoring that inner voice. *Intuition* is our guardian angel!

If you want love in your home, it must *first* begin *inside of you!* We know what makes us feel peaceful. We know what makes us happy. We must go where that peace is. We must go where we find heaven on earth. It's always right where we already are. It will show up when we actually begin giving ourselves random acts of kindness on a daily basis, which is usually by doing the things we *really love to do anyway.*

If we are constantly surrounded by people who think in a harmful and destructive manner, then we may unfortunately have a difficult time finding peace within our own heart. We must clean house (in our own minds) first! Sometimes there's so much clutter in our lives that we can't even see clearly enough to enjoy each moment of our day. Take a look to see what's cluttering your life, (people; endless job situations; objects, trash). Only you can answer the question of what's *not* working! Only you can get rid of the disorder, chaos and confusion now. Once you do...Never look back! Remember to be responsible as you make changes in your life!

We, as conscious individuals, have the choice to live our lives lovingly, satisfactorily, healthfully, and peacefully by sharing our loving heart with people all over the planet. As we begin to love and nurture our own heart first, only then can we carry it further to our mates and families, *then* with our next-door neighbors and co-workers, and finally the world.

If someone is hurting you, say to him or her directly, "I'm feeling hurt...Do you have a need to antagonize me?" If someone tries to manipulate you into doing something you know is wrong in your heart, then ask him or her directly... *"Do you feel the need to drag me into something that is against my better judgment?"* Remember...never accuse!

We have a choice as well as a responsibility to live out our lives from this day forward in harmony. Harmony *always* starts in our own hearts, and only then can it radiate outward. Remember that we *always* have choices in *everything* we do.

We don't need to be paranoid about "who is out to get us." We simply need to keep our eyes and ears open to all possibilities of *what's so in our lives.* The *truth* is already in each of us. Sometimes it's buried so deep within, and covered over with lies, that the challenge seems to be in *reaching* the truth. But your truth is always there.

Sometimes change can be painful. Maybe a change that needs to occur involves our life partners, job situation, or moving to a different area. Just pay attention and *feel* what's been draining you of your life force and energy.

Lately, I've noticed intense discomfort, upheaval, and unrest in the world. It's as if something has been brewing. If you throw into that pot...fear, apprehension, greed, panic, suffering, depression, mistrust, and manipulation...we're in big trouble! Now, since we have a choice, we can participate, cooperate, and align with this nonsense and fear, or we can go on about our lives on a daily basis and enjoy each moment. Personally, I'm up for living each day as if it's my last.

We're each on our own journey or mission in life. What's your itinerary? Mother Theresa's was obvious. When asked how she was able to help so many people in the world, her reply was, "by helping one person at a time." It seemed so easy for her, but that's only because she never looked past the *present moment*. She lived each minute as if it were her last. Most people don't know that she was born into an extremely wealthy family, but walked away from the opulence. There's nothing wrong with financial prosperity…but a world of luxury was simply not her calling.

How do *you* make a difference in the world? If you're not sure, just do what makes you really happy, and you'll end up leaving a trail of smiles behind you wherever you go. Don't take my word for it…just try it! We know there are no accidents in life, and everything happens for a reason. So trust in the universe, and listen. You'll always be lead to the place you're supposed to be next. The perfect people will always show up, who will lead you at least one step closer to your dreams and goals.

James Redfield wrote in his book *The Celestine Prophecy* that there are control issues *or* dramas we use in life to get what we want by *manipulating the energy* of others. We do this either by using aggression or by being passive.

The process of finding your true spiritual identity involves looking at your whole life as one long story, trying to find a higher meaning. We need to learn to bring our control issues and dramas into *full consciousness* before we can move forward in our lives. Mr. Redfield says that it is always in relation to our family members that we develop any of our 4 particular dramas. They are intimidator, interrogator, poor me, and aloof.

INTIMIDATOR = is someone who plays the bully, thug or heavy, so that you feel belittled, humiliated, ashamed, embarrassed and even stupid.

<u>INTERROGATOR</u> = is someone who asks you a lot of questions in order to ultimately find something *wrong* with you.

<u>POOR ME</u> = is the victim or underdog who lives his life by making sacrifices, sometimes at *your* expense.

<u>ALOOF</u> = is someone who acts distant, remote, detached, or indifferent.

He also says that playing any or all of these roles is *always* about "gaining energy from others," because most people don't know how else to *receive* energy... let alone generate it!

After reading his book, I've learned to walk in my own backyard and deeply breathe in *the energy of nature.* One of the techniques I use is to consciously breathe in the life force and energy of the birds, the trees, the flowers, the grass, and the sky. Of course, depending where you live in the world, some places have more energy to draw from. A forest with hundred year-old trees would probably have more life force than a bulb that was planted a year ago. You can go to a nursery, or be driving down the road and be able to breathe in nature and renew your energy level. I do this many times on a daily basis. It's become such a habit I don't even need to think about it any more. This is one of the greatest methods I've ever found to *continuously* feel centered and balanced. It's a form of yoga and meditation that works anywhere, anytime. Even if I know I'll be speaking in front of five thousand people, I just keep breathing in the life force of nature. Sometimes it might be a potted plant in a hotel lobby, if that's all I have to draw from!

Whenever you are around aggressive or manipulative people, you may feel a weakness take over. Unless you are paying attention to what's happening, you can be drained in a matter of seconds. Someone can simply walk into a room, and you can be either energized *or* zapped! All you need to do is *be aware* and recognize the role that people are playing, and you can continue to come from a loving space. This is so powerful!

These days, if anyone even comes close to me that seems to be drawing on my energy, I will excuse myself and walk away in a second! If someone calls me on the phone and begins to extract my energy level, I will politely excuse myself and get off the phone and immediately begin to re-energize myself *by using the life force in the environment.* Remember to...BREATHE!

I promise that once you get in the habit of extracting and refilling your life force from nature, instead of humans, **your life will change!** You will walk around feeling alert, vibrant, energetic, and feeling the best you possibly can. I do want to point out that the foods you eat also play a tremendous role in the way you feel. I'll discuss that in great detail in the chapter on food, diet and exercise.

Every human, (whether they are conscious of it or not), *demonstrates by "what they do",* how he or she thinks how people are "supposed" to live. Once you become *unencumbered from your past,* you can discover your spirituality and find your true nature of adventure and fulfillment. We need to discover who we really are and then move on to our real life purpose. At some level we know that life's meaning is to go beyond and rise above our past conditioning and move our life forward.

You are where you are, because you need to continue the process to evolve, develop, and expand to the next path or level of your life. If you pay attention to everyone around you, at each moment, you will grow at a much more rapid pace, excelling ultimately to peace, harmony, and love energy. When we consciously learn to progress forward using the energy and life-force of nature, rather than other humans, we have then found the true key to inner peace, joy, and happiness, and wake up to who we really are.

Once you learn a lesson, there is no way to erase that knowledge. You can no longer go back to the poor me syndrome. Your new way of looking, feeling, and being are transformed to a light-hearted buoyancy, and you float through life, feeling more in love and more present than ever before.

I can honestly tell you that I never used to enjoy the ride, or the process it took to reach new levels in my life. But today, I watch it unfold, as if it were the layers of an onion, gradually unraveling and revealing new surfaces that are unrecognizable and yet delightful to behold. Allowing yourself the freedom of exploring the deepest levels of your character and personality, is a gift. Only through this *process of discovery* will you find your *true identity.*

If your life is full of effort and pain, that's a sign it's time for a change. So keep examining and exploring your heart. Allow yourself to transform into what feels good and true. Each day, strive for your own personal best...because this is where *freedom* is!

If you're really fed up with the direction your life has taken, you'll find such peace when you allow yourself to *be, do,* and *have* anything and everything that you *know* you want in life. You can always change course at any time, so to stay on track, keep *checking in* with yourself.

Finding out who you really are, is *absolutely* worth your time and effort. The only thing that stops you from having what you want in life is *you*! Go ahead...find your truth! You will uncover your essence and your authentic spirit once your journey begins. The real fun is in the pursuit!

In some cases, the changes that have to be made in a person's life are so drastic that the transition or transformation may be painful, but the results and payoff are definitely worth your time and effort. In other cases, change may be as simple as going into a room, closing your eyes and going deep within, rather than trying to figure things out. Most of us are so busy being in our *heads* instead of our *hearts* that we don't stop long enough to just let things be.

The day that you enjoy you're own company, more than anyone else's, is a very special day. The day that you love "who" you see in the mirror is the day you truly wake up to "who" you *really* were meant to be.

I've had to learn to *design* my existence, by choosing role models who are appealing. It's enabled me to enjoy life to it's fullest. I strive to be the best person available at every given moment...I trust me...I like me...I have integrity. I believe this is more important than caring about what other people think anymore.

Although I love people, I've had to become more aware and alert, because of the occasional deceitful people who occasionally show up! Sometimes people just say what they think you want to hear, rather than be honest and tell you their truth. Even when they do tell their truth, they sometimes do it viciously. Be smart...for you were blessed with so much!

As a young adult teenager, my mother taught me to create my living space as if it were my castle. It didn't have to be elaborate...it simply needed to represent my lifestyle, my moods, and to accommodate what I like to do in life. Whether I lived in a shack, a studio apartment or a 6,000 sq. foot home wasn't the point. The point is...to create an inner world of comfort and enjoyment that nurtures and enhances me to be the best possible human being I can be.

I believe we all have something unique and special to contribute to the world. Even Osama bin Laden's evil ways contributed greatly to our love of life. At least we now know who the enemy is. It's not our neighbor's of different color or religion or nationality. It's the individual who wishes to purposefully inflict pain on others. It's the person who spreads fear, evil, and terror.

When you look in the mirror, which person are you today? Are you "loving" toward yourself and others? Do you create fear and disharmony wherever you go? How do you show up in the world? How do you carry yourself? What are you choosing for yourself? Are you making contributions to yourself and others? What difference would it make if you were gone?

If you really want to be the best possible *you*, which means living your dreams by design...take a look to see what friends and jobs you *have* and *do* in your life. I only choose to have people in my life who walk their talk, are supportive, and contribute by communicating their honesty and point of view without dumping or vomiting their words all over me. As for yourself... *"Who* are you letting in and, are you living your dreams *by design?"*

Even with the huge financial debt I incurred due to some foolish decisions I made, life rarely weighs negatively on me anymore.

Imagine what it would feel like to wake up happy *everyday*. Anyone can join in my fun, but I get to pick and choose whom I wish to let into my inner-sanctum, because I always re-design my life on a daily basis. We all have the freedom to do the same.

"Imagine if we lived in a world where the entire human race
Consciously attempted to bring out the best in others,
Rather than to have power over them.
Everyone's energy level and
Depth of evolvement and involvement would be increased.

We could permit our intuition to take over
Which would allow us to always do what we wanted to do,
Whenever we wanted to do it.

Imagine harmoniously living in a world
Where security comes from within,
Rather than worrying and wondering
How much the neighbors have.

"Imagine a world where consumption was never excessive
Because we had no need to hoard for the future.
Our own evolution would be gratifying in and of itself
Because of the natural differences that we would be
Contributing in the world,
Just by being ourselves!"

"Imagine all encounters being meaningful and significant,
Without need for manipulation
And/or greed on anyone's behalf.
Significantly touching and altering people's futures
Just by chance meetings.

Because of all ancestral beliefs and input over the centuries,
We now have the opportunity to choose freely
A future of bliss and a conscious evolution of harmony."

- James Redfield

– IF I HAD MY LIFE TO LIVE OVER –

- By Erma Bombeck

(Written after she found out she was diagnosed with cancer.)

"I would have gone to bed when I was sick instead of pretending the earth would go into a holding pattern if I weren't there for the day.

I would have burned the pink candle sculpted like a rose before it melted in storage.

I would have talked less and listened more.

I would have invited friends over to dinner even if the carpet was stained or the sofa faded.

I would have eaten the popcorn in the 'good' living room and worried much less about the dirt when someone wanted to light a fire in the fireplace.

I would have taken the time to listen to my grandfather ramble about his youth.

I would have shared more of the responsibility carried by my husband.

I would never have insisted the car windows be rolled up on a summer day because my hair had just been teased and sprayed.

I would have cried & laughed less while watching television, yet cried more while watching life.

I would have sat on the lawn and not cared about grass stains.

I would never have bought anything just because it was practical, wouldn't show soil, or was guaranteed to last a lifetime.

Instead of wishing away nine months of pregnancy, I'd have cherished every moment and realized that the wonderment growing inside me was the only chance in life to assist God in a miracle.

When my kids kissed me impetuously, I would never have said..."Later. Now go get washed up for dinner." There would have been more "I love you's."

But mostly, given another shot at life, I would seize every minute...look at it and really see it, live it, and never give it back. I'd stop sweating the small stuff.

Don't worry about who doesn't like you, who has more, or who's doing what. Instead, let's cherish the relationships we have with those who do love us.

Let's think about what God has blessed us with already...and what we are doing each day to promote ourselves mentally, physically and emotionally."

Erma...Thank you for giving me the humorous relief I needed in a much too serious and crazy world! - J'en El

Relationships...All of Life is Based on Relationships! Learn How to Turn All <u>Your</u> Relationships Into Fulfilling Ones!

The Source of All Relationships:

This is an extraordinarily important chapter, because everything we do in life will ultimately be determined by the quality of our relationships. With those we connect and link up with; work with; make love with; join; affiliate; companion with; team up and associate with, etc; people from all over the world on a second-to-minute-to-hourly basis since our conception. Even in our mother's womb, we are exposed to sensations from the outside world.

Our very character is determined:

- By who brought us into the world.
- By the attitude and reception of the doctors and nurses who delivered us.
- By the way our parents embraced and interacted with us.
- By the religion instilled in us.
- By the traditional culture and beliefs that were incorporated into us.
- By the way our teachers perceived and encouraged us.
- By the babysitters, co-workers, neighbors, family, friends, spouses, books, seminar leaders, newspapers, internet, email, cassettes, videos, DVDs...and the list goes on!

With all of this input, infiltrated into our core since birth, how do we learn to *authentically* relate to people in our own homes, schools, neighborhoods, jobs, and with every Tom, Dick, and Osama who comes along?

Subliminally, most of us are self-righteously, pre-judging *people, places,* and *things,* because we just "know" we're *right!* Our psyche has literally become saturated with different points of views. If it were just left at that, life would be fine. The problem with having a point of view (which we all do) is that most people think they *are* their point of view, therefore, they *need* to *be right.* If you insist on being *right,* then that would have to make someone else *wrong!*

Unfortunately...people with huge egos have been known to cause wars. People who display these massive egos usually experience such underlying *fear,* that they have a vested interest in appearing *reasonable, rational,* and *impartial.* If they were caught doing something that even resembles the appearance of looking irrational *or* suspicious, it would mean their gig is up. In their minds, they'd have to protect themselves from appearing absurd at any cost. In their own mind, they would cease to exist in a hierarchical power structure. Their own subconscious thoughts would take them down, for they exist on manipulating others, and we know people who have the need to manipulate are terrified below the surface. It all goes back to *the need to be right.*

Think about it...Hitler just *knew* he was right. But when the invasion came, he disappeared into thin air. He ceased to exist as Hitler, as we knew him. The gig was up!

Osama just *knew* he was right. But when the troops showed up, he disappeared into thin air. He ceased to exist as Osama, as we knew him. The "power is gone" if you're caught exploiting and then have the need to *hide out.* If you can't openly do something, than look within to see what you have to hide!

Years of input, feedback, and counseling teach most of us to be of the opinion that we are *right!* We all know that this doesn't make something "so," just because we were taught a certain way! Remember...there's almost *always* more than one way to see *or* solve a situation. Not just your way!

My friend Teddy could not find his gold chain. It was a family heirloom, which made it even more valuable to him. Teddy traced back (in his mind), when he last remembered wearing the chain. "I took it off when I went to play ball, and I saw a guy named James hanging around my belongings. I know he took it! That's the only possible solution," said Teddy, as his tension grew. Before long, Teddy went through a lot of different verbal scenarios that went from "I'm gonna' kill that guy," to "I never trusted him anyway," to " Oh my God...I just found my gold chain!" Finally, he came to me saying that he needed to keep a closer watch on his thinking. The light had gone on!

Here's a perfect example of someone who just *knew* he was *right* about "who snatched his gold necklace." He was ready to destroy a lifelong friendship because of his suspicious nature and by jumping to conclusions, rather than to investigate the situation. What would you have done if you were in Teddy's position?

We assume so much in life. People are killed everyday because of egos, subconscious beliefs, naiveté, foolishness, fear, madness, ignorance, malice and the need to be right. Ego is just *fear.* Some people are even *killed* in the "name of love." All of these things can be so destructive.

Some individuals are like high explosives, walking around, just waiting for an *incident* to occur. Whether the incident is a loving or volatile one, depends on their past programming or chemistry, which interact and go back to our ancestral heritage.

To end war and hatred...*judgments* and *assumptions* must cease! True inquiry must begin! If love and harmony are to exist, they must begin in our own hearts and homes first. In relating to people, *especially* with diverse cultures and backgrounds, we need to expand our consciousness and be less judgmental. It is unfair as well as stupid and dangerous to pass judgment on anyone.

If you married the person you went to school with, of the same age and religion who happened to live next door, you would most likely see eye-to-eye on most issues. On the other hand, you may have a very limited way of seeing the world...primarily because you never left your own backyard and you have nothing to compare anything to.

If you married someone with an extreme difference of age, who was born and raised in a different country, then agreeing on how to raise your children may become a major issue. Add to that, the diversification of religion, belief systems and political differences, you may have even greater challenges. You may not even make it through the first year. On the other hand, maybe your diverse background and worldliness allows you to accept and understand these differences, so that you and your mate may communicate through it, and last a lifetime together in love, peace and harmony.

94

If you're looking for a specific *formula,* then you may be in trouble. I will give guidelines that are fairly standard and basic, but they are still nonetheless of the utmost importance in maintaining a respectful, loving, lasting relationship. Just remember, when you get involved with *anyone,* you are *both* bringing with you, your entire ancestral history. From that point of view, how could anyone *ever* get along if they had the *need to be right?*

When I found out that attachment to and identification with *different points of views* actually create wars, I knew my patterns of thinking and relating in the world needed changing in order to maintain peace. It's for this very reason that my mate and I are still together. We realized very quickly that if our relationship was to have any chance of lasting, we both must learn to be flexible and respectful of the other's thoughts, and never to judge the other or make them wrong for their point of view about anything.

No one needs to sell out his or her belief. We simply need to have rational and civilized discussions and conversations about what we were taught, without anger or self-righteousness. There's never any need for an argument. These days, we are both able to surrender while engaged in conversations and, remain open minded to other possibilities that may exist in the world. This wasn't always the case! We had to give up hollering and arguing. There's just *nothing* to argue about...there are simply different ways of seeing.

The factor that has changed in my home is that neither my mate nor I have the need to be *right* about *anything* anymore. If I feel really strongly about something, I kid around with him and say "I accept your apology" in a very loving, playful way. We now get to laugh about a lot of issues. How can anyone be *serious* about being right in this very controversial world that we live in today? There are just too many variables in life, to get angry about anything.

My favorite flavor ice cream is French Vanilla. I know it sounds boring to a lot of people, but that doesn't change the fact that my favorite is French Vanilla! I actually remember a friend of mine trying to talk me into loving his favorite flavor more, just because mine was so basic and boring to him. How silly is that? If it's not going to hurt anyone, let people think what they want. It's none of our business. The only time it becomes our business is if it's destructive to other people, or to the well-being of the planet.

When relating to people, we need to go into situations with our eyes wide open and *never* with desperation! Did you ever notice that the very thing you loved about someone when you met him or her is usually the very thing that ends up bugging you later on? This always used to bewilder me. As I look back, what really astonishes me now, is that I was foolish and insecure enough to fall for the deceit or dishonesty in others. This is why we need to kiss a lot of frogs before we find a Prince or Princess. Take time to get to know people...*really* know them. "'Til death due us part" can be an eternity with the wrong partner.

I've been told..."where we left off with our parents and last mate, is precisely where we pick up in our *current* relationship." This is why it's imperative to clean up our messes along the way. Honest, responsible communication will continuously pave a clear path, ultimately avoiding trails of destruction, which will lead to a more desirable and mature relationship.

I don't think most of us set out in life to leave a *trail of destruction*, but somehow, most of us have managed to do just that. The good news is that most of the destruction is caused by ignorance which simply means *not knowing, inexperienced* or *unaware*. If this is true, that means we need *to find the mess we made and clean it up.* This usually involves deep introspection and soul searching. But how do we locate the entire trail of destruction we've created throughout our lifetime, when it seems so endless and huge.

I usually go into a deep breathing meditation with a legal sized pad and begin writing as thoughts come up. Eventually, you will remember *who* you've hurt in life. The list of casualties may take years to complete. Some of the terrible things we've done are hidden away in the deep crevices of our soul and cells. However, one day, someone does something to you and you have what Werner Erhard calls a "stack attack."

All of a sudden you remember something buried away that happened 38 years ago, or when you were 12 years old and you bullied the kid next door, or vice versa. Whatever it is, it will eventually come up. As it does, you have a few choices. You can call, write, or email the person you harmed and apologize. If you are unable to locate the person, or they're deceased, then write them a letter. Tell them how truly sorry you are for calling them names; or deceiving them; or hitting them; or gossiping about them; or going behind their back; or running around on them. Whatever it is, clean it up! I've been informed that this takes place in the 12-step program in *Alcoholic's Anonymous.*

Apologizing to people you've hurt will not only make them feel wonderful and maybe change their life...but "their forgiveness" *will release you* to move on and begin with a fresh, clean slate. It's also important that you forgive yourself for doing such mean things to others. Remember that you were ignorant and lacked some of the information you needed to do things in a polite and courteous way. By the way, if you've hurt so many people that it would take a lifetime to reach them all, then pray for forgiveness after writing it all down and remember to absolve yourself. Now, you can move on with your new life. Go ahead now...forgive yourself...allow yourself to receive everything you've ever wanted and dreamt of. You are so worth it!

You know the phrase..."Don't throw your pearls to swine!" I've learned to observe *by* watching *what* people *do*, and, if at all possible, I try to find something good in them. Interact with whomever you wish, but *pay attention.* Just because you like someone, or they seem to like you back doesn't mean that you take him or her home with you.

Before I would ever let anyone into my life in a live-in or intimate situation, I really want to know if I *like* that person as a true friend above and beyond anything else. A person's *actions,* speaks volumes! Ultimately, I don't listen to what people say. To me, the bottom line is what a person *does!* I've found out over the years that talk is cheap. Think about it...if you wait to see if people take action and actually *do what they say...*rather than simply *talk about doing something,* then you won't have to live in expectation of something possibly occurring.

To live in *expectation*, you will usually be let down in one form or another. By just hanging out and observing, you can save yourself a LOT of grief by *not* setting yourself up for hurt and disappointment.

It takes time to *truly* get to know another person. Sure, occasionally, it feels like "love at first sight," but that chemistry might be coming from lust, craving, hope, longing, desire, passion, yearnings, or even loneliness or survival. How do we know the difference? If you give a person enough rope, they will usually hang themselves. Wait and see... *without expectations*! It's better to find out *now* who the person is, than consuming days, months, years, or even your entire life by becoming intimate *first* and then finding out later on that he or she is the villain.

My friend Dr. Koichi Nakamura said that we must get to know another before making a commitment. He said that it takes at least a year to see all sides of a person. What's the hurry anyway? Why not just enjoy the journey?

Look at life as a smorgasbord where people are the menu. To talk and listen is to taste the flavor of another. Do more listening and watching if you really wish to see another's true nature. It always shows up. If you *ever* have a vested interest in the outcome of a relationship, then you probably won't allow yourself to experience the truth about the other person. Because, when we're desperate for something to happen, we usually only see what we want to see.

If you keep an open mind *the first year*, and have no expectations, this will save you so much anguish, grief, agony, heartache, distress, suffering, and possibly even depression. This allows you time to become true friends first. *True friendship* gives people a stronger foundation, as well as something to fall back on when things get rough... and they will get rough!

Don't believe old "wives' tales"... you won't become an *old maid* if you're not married by a certain age. Times have changed, and a lot of people have changed their priorities! Be careful what you ask for, because it surely will come. Where do you draw the line for yourself? What exactly is your life worth? What do you really *love* to do? Get very clear, be specific, and live your dreams. When you least expect it, the right person will be magnetized to your gorgeous energy. Remember not to pick up any "free-loaders" along the way! Some people are like parasites. You give...they take! Make sure you're relationships are contributing *positively* to everyone involved.

If you want any relationship to be successful, you must first understand that *everyone* thinks *differently!* Of course there will be plenty of overlapping similarities. Some times it's eerie, just how similar we are to certain people, but, nonetheless, no two people think identically! The closest you'll ever find is in a twin or a clone, which are phenomenons in and of themselves.

If no two people think alike, then we need to take into consideration that *the differences we do have,* will show up sooner or later. So, we must learn to honor, respect, and allow those differences to remain present, as well as keep our eyes open to what's really going on. Since we already know we can't change people, we must walk away when the differences are so extreme and extensive, that we can no longer function at full capacity. Out of respect for yourself, don't lie about what the truth really is. Especially if you're already in a relationship where children are involved, and *abuse* comes into play. That's when we **must** walk away. Don't ever stay "for the children," because the children always see what you do, and they will most likely follow in your footsteps. The more co-dependent you are with your partner, the more dysfunctional your children will become.

Be sure to make a list and write down all of the qualities that you desire your mate to possess. Good looks are nice, but they're irrelevant over time. Be sure to include the following affirmation: I **give thanks that this wonderful person is now in my life!** Attract your perfect mate through positive affirmations and wholesome thoughts.

If we look at the evolution of mankind over the centuries, everyone seems to have had the "ideal" *unique thought* as to what a perfect relationship would look like. Once we expand our perception of the world, the variety of cultures is astounding. In one country, you'll see women as subservient. In other cultures, mothers are the matriarchal leaders and treated as goddesses. In other parts of the

99

world, women aren't allowed to be in public without a male figure, and even when she is, she's not allowed to show her face.

Another thing you'll see in some cultures is that citizens aren't allowed to read books or listen to music. If they're caught...they'll be killed! This brings a whole new meaning to *extreme* points of views!

You can search to the ends of the earth and very likely come up with thousands of ideas as to how different cultures *relate* with the opposite sex, as well as the different taboos, restrictions, and beliefs about love and mankind.

Since the age of 4, I was intrigued at the way men and women related in *my* limited world. As a young adult, I continued to closely monitor the mating rituals of our society. Here's what I see! Some people use their sexuality to lure a mate. Some use their Epicurean skills in the kitchen. Some use their intellect and educational background as bait. Some people allure with the finest perfumes and colognes. Some wear extravagant clothing and accessories to attract a mate. Some males tempt with expensive cars, gifts, and money to seduce their potential live-in fare of the evening, *or* potential mother of their children.

In some cultures, men will marry an immaculate person to become the mother of their children and have sexual encounters on the side. Some women choose men who will be able to take care of their financial needs throughout life, thus dating and marrying for money. We can of course never forget about the older, wealthier men who marry the gorgeous young "arm candy babes." They both are caught in the "status symbol" relationship. She gets to live opulently and he gets a "trophy" to show off wherever he goes. Who knows...maybe that is a win-win situation...it's not for us to judge.

Personally, I'd rather be whole and complete within myself first, so that I can be with my mate, simply because we enjoy each other's company. I don't want to be with anyone, *ever* just because I need something from him or her. Also, I don't want to have to act *or* look *or* be a certain way, just so he'll love me.

I remember seeing a movie called *"The Man Who Loved Women"* starring Burt Reynolds. He saw a woman with the most beautiful legs he had ever seen. He said that he was afraid to speak with her because *"What if the top half didn't match the bottom half."* Who knows *why* people get together or what makes them happy? My whole point is that even though there is no magic formula for creating the *perfect* relationship, we need to take a look at what we were *taught*, which is usually what we *believe* and assume to be accurate.

Here's where the challenges come in. In the real world, especially with today's technology, it's so easy to meet people "out of the neighborhood," with entirely different cultures and beliefs. There's no way that you could possibly *ever* know what another person is thinking, and we know that we're never willing to *assume.* So what do we do? We ask questions *now...* before it's too late. I believe we know in the first minutes, days, or weeks, if a person is *not* for us, but *out of desperation* we try to make something fit that doesn't, like pushing a circular object into a square opening.

What *standards* have you set in your mind for the *ideal* mate? Your criteria may be *off the chart.* In which case, no one will ever be good enough for you. The other side of that coin is that maybe you haven't set your standards high enough. Remember that **you deserve the very best**, so think big and live your dreams!

I used to worry if a person would become aggravated, annoyed, insulted or offended with any of my *comments* or *questions.* Now, I just speak to everyone in the same tone. If they like me, fine. If they don't, that's fine also. I know I can't please the world...so I finally stopped trying. Life has become so much easier *and* a lot more fun, since I learned to live in the moment. If I feel like someone is trying to put me down, or not accepting me for who I am, then I courteously excuse myself and walk away. I wish I had learned to do that earlier in life. I would have saved a lot of precious time.

Trying to *please the world* is just too heavy of a weight to carry around. All we can do is be our *best* without trying to impress. Be your true authentic self. If someone loves you for *who* you are, then great! If they don't...there are just too many other wonderful people all over the world to be wasting your time where you're not loved or appreciated. Remember to be responsible with everything you do in life, *especially* when you are making significant changes. Remember, never accuse people...always inquire!

I keep myself surrounded by people who have *opened themselves* to the world. I appreciate people who are *private*, but people who appear *secretive* repel me. There's a tremendous difference. *Privacy* helps create balance and self-control. To be *secretive* is when someone appears sneaky as if something is being concealed. I will simply *not* be around *anyone* who constantly disturbs my balance. If I feel annoyed or badgered in someone's presence, then I'm out of there. If I hear a bunch of whining or complaining, I'm out of there! Life is much too short to harbor grief and aggravation.

We never need to be paranoid about situations we're in. Just walk away from matters that don't serve you or others, or especially situations that don't *feel* right. You're inner voice will always guide you to move away and be in the right place at the right time. You may not always realize *why* you *are* where you currently are at a certain time, but later on in our lives, *everything* naturally connects and fits together, appearing as if there was a master plan all along.

After a while, you will always naturally know what to do next, because following your instincts will have become a habit and a pattern from reading this book and/or listening to the "**Finding Comfort**" CD over and over. We can condition ourselves to be, do, and have almost anything in life.

Conditioning
Is simply creating a *state of being*
Where you prepare yourself to
Become one with your body, mind, spirit, and soul,
And everything you do
Begins to *compatibly resonate with life*
As a *habit* from that moment on...
Which is *the* moment
When you say
"It Is So," and so it is.

- J'en El

It's just a fact that some people will be secretive and have hidden agendas, so "go where they're not!" I've mentioned throughout this book that words can be like sharp weapons, so we must be appropriate in our communications and responsible for our actions. People don't seem to do too well when they find out that you had a hidden agenda, so be up front with everyone right from the start.

With today's modern and massive technology that surrounds us 24/7, we're dealing with the entire planet...Internet, cell phones, and the airlines connect us with anyone in the world instantly. So with literally millions of great people in this world, you *must know* that you will resonate naturally with *at least* one other human on the planet. If you don't, then maybe your standards *are* simply unrealistic. There are *no* perfect humans. They just don't exist. All of us have flaws. Why would you even want to subject yourself to *perfection* anyway? To be perfect can be tiresome and even boring. Diversity is what keeps life interesting. Having "standards of excellence" is an entirely different matter, which I consider admirable.

Go ahead...make a list of your ideal mate, and be specific! Ask for what you want and you just might get it! Now...come back to reality and cross off the ridiculous. Only leave the things on the list, that *really* matter to you, forgetting what society taught you...that you *"should"* have. What would make you really content and joyful? Would he or she be *the one* if the two of you lived on a desert island, and money was of no concern?

When you find the right person, you'll always be able to *feel* when love is present and *mutual*. Words aren't even necessary. It's the *actions* that tell all! Be conscious before you say... *"I do!"* As I said, *"'Til death do us part" can seem like an eternity when you're with the wrong partner!* If you must speak, in my experience, one of the sweetest things you can say to someone is *"I'm glad you're here"*...and mean it! To me... *"I'm glad you're here"* is even more delightful than "I love you."

From my point of view...*love is visible*. Maya Angelou wears the look of love. Oprah wears the look of love. Another example of *visible love* was seeing the faces of Ron Goldman's dad and sister throughout the *"OJ trial."* What a gorgeous family to behold. What a tragedy...yet what an inspiration! Every *look* they wore had love written all over it. There's a peace and contentment that overrides and surpasses all else. It's the look of being grateful for what you already have vs. a *longing* for what may have been.

If you're in a relationship *where you can't* "live and let live," then you're with the wrong person. We must never be foolish enough to believe that we can *change* another human being. If you're not happy in your current situation, then you're wasting your life and your time here on earth. Make something happen! It's time you know and recognize that you're just too good for nonsense. Don't always wait to let things simply fall where they may...or you could miss out on a lot of living. It's perfectly okay *right now* for you to reprogram yourself by beginning to create new habits.

If it's true that our own needs must be met before we can give to anyone else, then it's probably a wise idea to start loving yourself right now. We must stop looking to others to live our life for us. Go ahead, rescue yourself before it's too late. Take charge right now and begin to design your new life. Allow yourself to have everything you've ever wanted. If you only knew how *really worth it* you are, you'd be wearing a smile of joy right now. Our divine creator just doesn't make junk.

Here's the perfect example of what *not* to do:

Many years ago, my best friend fell into a short-lived marriage at a very vulnerable time in her life. When she met a man 11 years younger from Guatemala, she became completely mesmerized. He was tall, dark, and handsome. He told her everything a woman longs to hear. Finally his alluring smile won her over...she was doomed! Beware of the hidden agenda!

He forgot to mention that he wasn't a citizen and needed a green card to stay in the country. She forgot to mention that she was worried about becoming an "old maid" if she wasn't married by the age of 30...she was already 31 which added a real time crunch to the situation. So together they united in what became a less than blissful matrimony. Within months, he became physically and verbally abusive. She obviously never thought this matter through entirely. Eventually...after he got his green card, she was lucky enough to sneak out of her own home in the middle of the night, for fear of losing her life. Eventually they got a divorce and lived happily ever after...after years of therapy and expense, of course.

In retrospect, we can look back on this matter as ridiculous and a total waste of time, except of course, for *the huge learning experience* for my friend. We can analyze the situation, but the bottom line is this. There was no communication on either of their parts. They each had hidden agendas. They both came from vastly differently cultural backgrounds and belief systems. She was totally won over by lust, hope, and fear. She thought she needed a husband to be okay in the world. He knew that he needed a green card to stay in the country. They both used each other to get what they wanted, rather than be honest, tell each other their beliefs and fears, and both ultimately paid a very high price. Can you see the irony here? They both probably could have gotten what they wanted without the pain and expense of *their lives* if they'd openly and honestly communicated. Our *sanity, happiness* and *life* are just too high of a price to pay for anything!

There's a certain *dependence* or *need* that seems to ride on the coattail of most relationships. This neediness stems from deep inner feelings of inadequacy, insufficiency and unworthiness. Being in a relationship can be wonderful. It can also bring up a lot of pain. Have you ever noticed who receives most of the insults and mistreatment in relationships? It's usually the significant other, the children, or other family members. Relationships can be notorious for all kinds of abuse, whether it's physical, mental, or verbal. Personally, I choose not to play in any of the above! There's no reason to allow abusive behavior *ever*! It's really pathetic to watch, *or* be a part of! If your significant other is *not* your best friend, you might want to ask yourself...why not? Best friends bring out the best in each other...not the worst!

Why is it that the very person who *should* receive the majority of respect, love, and admiration is getting the least amount? Once you truly respect yourself, you will *never* allow this to happen. *You will never* mistreat or abuse anyone, nor will you accept it from any other human being! It's just not tolerable, nor is there an excuse for it. If we all lived by this standard, there could be no wars. If abuse is going on in your life, then you must clean it up responsibly, or move on. If you've done everything in your power via communication and/or counseling, and nothing has changed, then sayonara, adios...I'm out of here! Move on...you owe it to yourself now!

We all know that fear is destructive. It creates anxiety, worry, grief, and panic, just to name a few. It's best to alleviate fear, before we enter into a romantic relationship. It's also best to be clear about who we are, and what we're passionate about in life.

In order to lessen our fear, we need to take the initial steps of *becoming, doing,* and *having* what we want in life. It's best when entering into a relationship to already be *complete* within your self, and not to *need* or *expect* anything from another person. To be dependent on someone already puts us into a *needy* situation.

It's best to enter into relationships *after* you've *done the work* and already healed yourself. *Co-dependency* is where we don't function very well without the other person, which tends to put us into the desperation, fear or needy category. These days, I steer clear of people who have the leech or pit-bull mentality. You know the ones who tend to suck you dry until there's nothing left.

I'd much prefer to be involved with someone just because I'm a better person when I'm with them, or simply because, we enjoy each other's company. I never want to be in a relationship where someone is there out of guilt or obligation.

We need to take care of ourselves. This is why I keep mentioning that we need to *do the work* first. This means in every aspect of our lives; mentally; physically; spiritually; and emotionally. There's a fine line between taking yourself seriously vs. being *serious.*

Do what you love.
Get out of your own way.
Put your needs first.
Put a smile back on your face

106

Don't look to others to put it there for you.
Take responsibility for the health,
Appearance and well-being of your body.
Know how to eat consciously.
Breathe deeply and deliberately.
Stimulate your flow of oxygen to promote well-being.
Know how to derive energy from nature,
Diversify your exercises.
Love who you see when you look in the mirror,
Before inviting others into your world.
Know that you are already whole and complete.
Be grateful for what you already have.
Know that taking care of you is not selfish,
It's being self-aware!

It's wonderful to be in love and feel nurtured, touched, cared for and caressed by others. I always welcome nurturing, however…I never look to anyone for nurturing or love. I nurture myself. This allows me to ultimately be whole and complete so I can be there for others, and yet welcome any nurturing that happens to come along, that anyone wishes to give.

<u>Here are a few of the affirmations that I use regularly…</u>

- I am always divinely guided to be in the right place at the right time.
- I always attract the perfect people who love contributing to my life and well-being, as I do for them.
- I am blessed to always receive everything that I ask for with gratitude.
- The perfect people, places and things are always placed on my path to contribute to my life in positive ways.
- My prayers and needs are always answered and met at the perfect time.
- Everything I do is easy and effortless, or with ease and grace.
- Everything I do is filled with love, joy and peace.

If you've been obsessing over the *"Knight In Shining Armor Syndrome,"* it's time to stop and let that go. Most of us have prayed and wished throughout our entire lives for the right person to come along, but in doing so, a lot of us have put our lives on hold in the process. "If only I had a mate who loves me." We need to stop that and move on. If that's what you've been doing, just know you're probably not loving yourself and taking care of your own needs enough.

Have you ever considered that if you're not currently in a committed relationship that maybe it's a *good thing*? It gives you more time to go within and find out who you really are and what you really love to do. After you experience the best of yourself, you can bring someone else into your world, someone that has *also* done the work. This will put you both on a level playing field. This is where contributions can be made to one another *and* to the world at new, higher levels of achievement.

Even with a mate, you can feel so alone at times. If your happiness depends on someone else, then it's really time for you to go within and figure out what you haven't been *giving to yourself.* We tend to withhold love from our*selves.* That's not a good idea. If you aren't gracious enough to take care of the little child that lives within your heart, then you will never be able to truly take care of anyone else in a responsible way. The truth is...your life depends on you taking charge and living your dreams out loud.

I used to be in love with the *idea* of romance...and in love with *love*! When I looked up the definition of romance its synonyms were "fiction" and "fantasy." Are we looking for something that doesn't exist, and maybe never existed except in our mind? Later in life, I was lucky enough to finally fall in love with myself, and I can never again sell out *who I am.* Once we really know something, we can't go back to the way things were.

Both my mate and I *always* know where the front door is. If he's not completely happy being with me then it would be better if he were to leave, and vice-versa. After many years, we've learned to compliment, celebrate, and respect one another instead of contradict and annoy the other.

In the "name of love," most of us weave vicious, cyclical webs until it *appears* as if there's no way out. Sometimes a person can be too much in love, and thus become blind. You can choose the *attitude* with which you go through situations!

If you feel *stuck* in a relationship, and haven't been able to work through your *circumstances*, then get help. Support for growth and healing is *always* available, just by asking. Get out of your own way and take charge of your life now by aligning with your higher self and your limitless imagination.

Remove the self-inflicted restrictions and fly! Remember to get out of your own way. Can you afford to let *fear* hold you back any longer? Relationships are much easier and more likely to last when you both *individually* have a firm foundation, hopefully *before* entering into the relationship. Also, it's always best to be *friends* before becoming intimate.

<u>Here are a few SECRETS to a Successful Lasting Relationship</u>:

I notice that most people take *the basics* for granted once they've been involved for a while and the honeymoon phase is over. It's the common courtesies that will keep you together, like a simple thank you, *and* how was your day. Most importantly...either say "I love you" or "I'm so glad you're in my life," but not unless you mean it!

<u>Always stay in touch with the BASICS!</u>

Apologize if you've done something disrespectfully...
It doesn't mean you're wrong.
Never go to bed *angry* with anyone...
Especially your significant other.
Greet each other enthusiastically with love in your heart.

Touch and hug your mate with a smile.
Always tell the truth and ask for what you want,
In the most responsible, gentle, loving way.
Never accuse!

Always use positive conversation.
Don't hate or dread anything,
Or it will show on your face and in your actions.
Allow...rather than tolerate.

Let people be who they are!
We all have different points of views, needs and wants.
Be mentally and spiritually there for your mate whenever possible.
Ask for what you want.

Never take the other person for granted.
Grow together.
Inspire each other.
Respect each other.
Never treat the other like a doormat, or punching bag.

Give up control and drama.
Be Best Friends.
Never take the role of a *drill sergeant*.
Don't suffocate or stifle.
Laugh together.

Support each other to succeed in goals and dreams.
Make sure your mate feels *safe* around you *and* vice-versa.
Make sure your mate feels *important* around you and vice-versa
Just *be there* when you see they're down.

Listening is a courtesy...*advice* is not always necessary.
Make sure you're contributing to each other.
Smile without judgment.
Be patient...within reason.

Always watch what people do...*not* what they say!
Just care ...unless it's crippling to you or others.
No ego's allowed!

Just be a *mensch* (which in German means "human being.")
Mensch, in the Yiddish language, refers to an especially upright,
honorable, and decent person – a person of moral consequence and
stability.

Doing these things will allow your mate to know you're seeing them in a new, special way as if for the very first time, and not taking them for granted, or holding any old grudges.

If you have expectations or take the other for granted, you're destined to fail. You need to be friends' first if you want to have a long term, lasting, loving, relationship. You must also have a foundation of respect! Best friends grow together over time. Honest communication is how true friendships are born! No need to rush through or try to push things into place. Let things *flow* into place.

I regard everyone I currently deal with as a friend, especially and foremost my significant other. If I find out *any* of my friends can't be trusted, I'm out of there! My true friends count on me to succeed. That's what support looks like! True friends show appreciation to one another, tell each other the truth and are *kind* and loving to each other as well.

Don't ever keep anyone around who lies to you, or abuses you. If they do it once, shame on them. If they do it twice...shame on you! Be clear who your true friends are and aren't! To be in a relationship without games and egos, along with a foundation of mutual respect, is a beautiful thing to behold! Love is visible!

Be with people of similar interests. If you have nothing in common, it tends to make situations more awkward. If you love to golf, find someone who also loves to golf. If you love to travel, find someone who loves to travel. If you love to work out at the gym, find someone who understands the importance of oxygenating the body and weight training. If you're a vegetarian, then at least find someone who is conscious about their eating habits. You and your mate don't need to see eye to eye on everything. However, the things that are *most* important to you, should also be at least of a *similar* nature and interest to them.

A lot of the new comedy sitcoms on television, portrays couples having conversations where the wife is talking and the husband hasn't heard a word she says. I'd rather be without a mate if that were true of my relationship. What would be the point?

These fundamental similarities and common courtesies become so important over time. We need to *grow together in the same direction* to become life partners. It will make the difference of having a loving companion later in life, and growing together in the same direction, rather than growing apart. Also, when you're virtually on the same path, it's easier for you to assist each other in reaching your dreams and goals. One of the easiest ways to achieve growth in the same direction is to always be your *authentic* self from the moment you meet, *and* to maintain the courage to continue on your true path. Your journey throughout life will ultimately be much more enjoyable together through mutual support.

One day, I got a call from my mate on our adjoining cell phone. After a brief conversation, we hung up the phone. He forgot to engage his telephone keys in the *"lock"* position, and the redial button automatically called me right back without him knowing. My phone rang; I said hello; and what I heard made me laugh so long and so loud, that tears began to stream down my face.

I realized as I heard him whistle, and then hum, and then sing, and then yodel, that he obviously did not know that our phones had a connection. Because he was unaware of what had happened, I got to innocently eavesdrop. I heard a side of my mate I had never experienced in the 11 years that we had been together. At that moment, I realized that at the age of 56, he had never felt *safe* enough to tap into his innocence or unselfconsciousness around me. Can you imagine how stifled, constrained, and uptight, he must have felt at times in all of those years that we lived together under the same roof?

The next thing that happened turned my laughter into sadness. All of a sudden, his whistling, humming, singing, and yodeling ceased. Through the silence I heard his car stop and the disengaging sounds of his seat belt. I ran to the window, and sure enough, there he was, solemnly walking up the path to our front door.

He went from a happy, singing, yodeling guy to a somber, detached, and reserved person. I was so disturbed! I realized that in all of our years together, he just didn't feel relaxed enough around me to be playful. That realization hurt me so much, that I became overwhelmed with sadness. I told him what had occurred. I told him how I laughed 'til I cried. I told him how sorry it made me feel that I could be playful around him, but he never felt safe or confident enough to be that way around me. All of my comments were said without accusation, but I knew that if I didn't ask for what I wanted at that moment, that our relationship would be doomed.

Through the power of honest, responsible communication, we've been able to transform our relationship. You don't need to waste a lot of years to have what you want from your significant other. These days we compliment one another by allowing the other a safe space to be who we wish to be at any and every given moment. If you don't feel comfortable enough to be *authentic* and *playful around your mate,* then you're wasting you're limited time here on this planet.

My life partner and I are best friends who get to hang out together as we attain our goals in life. What could be better? Don't settle for a mate that doesn't support you. You'll be more approachable when you do the things you love to do in life anyway.

I've been taught to look at relationships as three circles, placed horizontally, overlapping, next to one another, side by side. The far right circle represents you. The far left circle represents your significant other. The adjoining center circle represents the two of you *together* as one. That's where you both share all of your love and devotion. In that center circle, you get to share all of the things that you enjoyed, learned, saw and experienced out in the world each day. If you don't do this, it's very easy for your relationship to stagnate. Make sure you both have separate, distinct, well-adjusted lives, so that when you do come together, it's joyful. Having some sort of outside life apart from one another is healthy as long as it's part-time and doesn't poison or separate the two of you.

For quite a few years, my mate and I somehow got caught up in the *"Couch potato syndrome."* We had been experiencing stagnation in our relationship for a long time. I finally joined an empowerment group for women. At that point in time, I felt like I regained my life. Then, he joined an empowerment group for men. This opened up a world of possibilities for we now both had outside interests which

113

brought us closer together. This enabled us to be on the same page in life and to do the same dance. We began to share fun stories at the end of each day. This brought vibrancy and spice back into our relationship. We've met couples and individuals who share the same interests, which has given our social life a boost in the right direction. We had temporarily forgotten *how fun it was* to get together with other people of like minds. Joy and laughter came back into our lives.

No matter how busy you become...get involved with *something* that makes you happy. Open new doors and get involved with life! You'll find paradise right in the heart of your own jungle, regardless of the circumstances.

If you're in a relationship and your mate is physically, mentally, or verbally abusive, get some help immediately. If you've both gone through counseling, and the abuse has continued...get out now while you're still alive. If they've made threats like "if you leave, I will kill you," then make serious arrangements quietly in advance and get yourself and your family to a safe haven. Safe houses are available everywhere. Phone books are full of listings for police departments, community centers, churches, and social service organizations. Make calls while your mate is not around so you can plan a safe escape. Abusers are *fools*, and that makes you not only a *victim*...but a *fool* as well...if you stay in that kind of relationship. Get out **now** while you're still alive! If there's no abuse in your relationship, then start finding what's *right* with your mate, instead of what's *wrong* with them.

Different Kinds of Love:

Human beings are multi-faceted. We're quite capable of loving more than one thing *or* one person at a time. This pertains to *everything;* occupations, jobs, hobbies, people, roles we play, types of music and instruments, skin care lines, hair colors, foods, and so on.

I've learned not only to *accept* change, but also to embrace and appreciate it. Life is just a re-circulation, re-distribution, and re-formation of *energy.* Now that I've chosen to greet each day with love in my heart I've learned to watch it *unfold* in amazement. It's all about *attitude* and how we choose to see things. My life was previously displayed as old boring *re-runs* from the past. Today, I choose *fun* instead.

I never really know how each day will turn out, but I've learned to go with the flow, as well as design and create each moment as it occurs. It's just about remembering to *check in* to see what you *feel* like doing.

I decided that if I stop taking things so seriously or personally, and I give up trying to hold or *force* things into place, that letting things unfold *naturally* would open up a world of *possibilities*. What could be more exciting! Exertion was just too painful. Make a tight fist and you'll see what I mean. I found that life is simply too short to force anything. Now, instead of trying, I just *do* what I want, and what feels natural. You might be asking...what does this have to do with relationships? I think, everything!

I love to be with different people for different reasons. Everyone brings something unique and distinct to the party of life. I have some of the most wonderful friends in the world. I adore my friends. If you're one of the people "I call friend," and you're reading this right now, you will automatically know who you are. You know...

   - Because as a friend, you've made contributions to my life.
   - Because you put a smile on my face.
   - Because you helped lift me out of darkness when I felt like I
     was sinking.

Because the world is so full of diversity, we get to pick and choose on a moment to moment basis what we wish to do, and with whom we wish to do it. We were born and blessed with *freedom*, to pick and choose anything and everything in life.

Different situations that occur on a daily basis will of course elicit different choices and different outcomes. I happen to use the most fabulous anti-aging skin care line available, however, occasionally I still like to alternate for a day or so to different products from a few different lines. Depending on *what* I've been doing and *where* I've been will determine which one is necessary on any given day. I mix and match different products, as it's fun to play and experiment.

I like to vary my schedule instead of falling into ruts and routines, so some days, I may wake up and wash my hair, while other days, I don't even comb my hair. Some days I put my hair in a ponytail. Some days I put a wig or hairpiece on. The point is…we get to alternate and play at life and *to make it up everyday*! Most people go through their days, living quiet lives of desperation, doing the same boring, monotonous things again and again. Different people add and contribute different things to our lives. They're all necessary in making us who we are. I've learned to *never* say "yes" to anyone or anything in my life anymore, without thinking it through first! Life is just too short to be wasting our precious time, and energy doing anything that we don't enjoy doing.

Are you depleting *or* contributing to the people you're in relationships with? We must learn to honor and allow people to be the way they are! We can't change them, so why bother trying. Just because we like someone and have a few similar interests, doesn't mean we have to take that person home and sleep with them…

- Where's the win *or* gain in your relationship?
- Why are you with this person?
- Do you bring out the best in each other?

We can find *fresh solutions* for any challenge that occurs. We just need to learn how to *see* situations differently on a daily basis and accept things as they are. In *accepting*…we grant, acknowledge, and permit people to *stay* the way they wish. If you try to change people, they'll usually resist, and in turn become defiant, aloof or resentful. Once this happens, it's hard to gain back their trust. If we simply live our life authentically and be a good example, they may *choose* to change by emulating what you're doing because it simply makes sense to them.

It's important to continuously stay clear and energized. When we *are energized*, we can see things more clearly *and* more easily empower others. As I mentioned earlier, the easiest way to attain energy is by breathing in deeply and consciously, using the higher sources of nature, such as the forest, trees, plant life, birds, rabbits, the sky, and animals…rather than sucking, draining, or depleting your friends, family and co-workers of all their life force. All things are more

116

enjoyable when we are getting what we need. A lot of our needs are met when we breathe in nature. This will lead to the purest and most meaningful conversations you will ever experience. When you are clear, you never have the need to be *right* about anything. When you don't have a need to be right, there is peace!

Learning how to communicate to people in a meaningful, eloquent way can be positively profound and life changing when we take responsibility. Most friction and conflicts can be worked through and dealt with when you both learn how to communicate *without blame*. It's irresponsible and an injustice *not* to *air your concerns*. Other people can get hurt if we remain silent. If you want to assist in killing off someone's spirit...just give them the silent treatment. Silence is **not** always golden! Clean, honest communication is vital. *Knowing* something is the easy part...*saying* it however can sometimes be difficult!

If someone makes the righteous statement..."I know how you always need to control and manipulate!"...Then they are *not* interested in your response, because they are negatively *accusing* you of something. This leaves no room for inquiry! They are simply holding you in old and negative thought patterns, which is rude and arrogant! Remember...if we see people in a *new way*, as if meeting for the first time, we could dissolve all judgment and remain *open*.

On the other hand, if a person says *"I feel as though I'm being manipulated when we're having a conversation, and it makes me feel sad,"* you'll notice there's no accusation there, as the person is simply speaking about the way they feel. This type of communication can give the other person food for thought, so that they can go inside themselves and examine what *their* truth is.

Is there anything other than to feel sad, hurt, pain, love, or happiness? Don't allow yourself to give up or shut down without claiming your share of happiness! This is your chance to *heal* situations that have been unresolved and most likely ...*uncomfortable* for so very long.

Keep breathing and staying in touch with your feelings. Re-group! Constantly tell yourself the truth. No accusations or make-wrongs *ever* on your part. Keep staying in touch with your truth. Don't let things fester. Constantly *clean up stuff* as it occurs, so that down the road, you won't have a "stack attack!"

To remain *clear* and *open*, I like to write things down, until the appropriate words and thoughts come to me. Then I communicate it as responsibly as possible to the other person involved. Sometimes, I don't always have the "happy ending" I had hoped for, but that's okay, because there are no mistakes in life, and sometimes we need to move on from certain situations. Remember…we are a "work in progress!"

It's very important that we *always* give people time to absorb, digest, and process our communication, so that they can in turn be responsible also. Everyone receives and processes information in a different way, so remember to give people the necessary *space* to get centered and focused after receiving your communication! Get outside and experiment, but be gentle and *always* loving.

Make sure that you choose a mate who is *already* kind, has high morals and integrity, and knows the difference between right and wrong. This will make life not only endurable for you, but also enjoyable for everyone involved. Make sure any person you enter into a relationship with is worth your time and energy. If not, why are you with them? You should be able to do just about anything with your life partner. My mate and I can floss our teeth in front of each other, color our hair, and even wear a facial mask. We don't want to hide or feel ashamed about anything that we do in life. We must also be clear about that *fine line* that crosses over the sexuality barrier and comfort zone. That's another book entirely, but the bottom line is make sure you also remain desirable, approachable, playful and sexy to your partner.

I want to know that I can ask my mate for assistance with anything, and that he'll be there for me. If he were unavailable most of the time, then what kind of relationship would or could we have? I am however, *always* very respectful of his time. I ask *if* and *when* he would be available to assist me. I never automatically assume that he should drop what he's doing at any given moment, unless of course there was a true emergency. Not only would that be rude, but it would be taking his time for granted, as if my time were more important than his, as well as having *expectations* on my part.

As long as I remain respectful of his time, then we can never fall into the *blame game* of "you never make time for me syndrome." Ask for what you want! Schedule quality time to be with your mate if you wish to remain life partners, because life is just already so full 24 hours of every single day. You can only "blame" if you had an original expectation about something to begin with. It takes continuous responsibility and maturity, to avoid pitfalls, and stop plunging into the same old boring, negative habits. I feel like I'm constantly taking alternate routes while maneuvering my way through life, and taking detours whenever I see a potential roadblock ahead. I believe this saves a lot of time and aggravation on everyone's part. A beautiful, mutual, *potential* relationship is around just about any corner just waiting to bloom. There are too many good people in the world to be hanging out with foolish ones.

So…what *is* love?

I guess it's different for a lot of people, but I do believe when you choose to spend time with someone and you both emerge to be a better person as a result…this is a truly wonderful thing!

Those 3 horizontal circles I previously mentioned…say it all. You see…if we continually have outside interests; and these interests help to stimulate our relationship, then we both grow as a result…instead of stagnate. If you both grow and reach new levels together, then you both, go back out into the world, and pick up new information, and grow some more. Once you get into this kind of cycle, your relationships will all be magical and exhilarating. Not to mention how they'll flourish.

Most of us tend to *assume* things about people, just because we've *heard* about specific things that they've done in their past. Just because you *hear* someone's story does not mean that you *know* him or her at all!

The important thing is to *see* who he or she evolves to be, while in your presence, and who you evolve to be in their presence. This will speak volumes!

119

As I mention throughout the book, we must be in relationships where we can take silent moments for ourselves without being hassled by anyone... *especially* our significant other. I could never take on a partner who didn't understand the importance of taking *and* making *personal* time, particularly for introspection. Introspection leads to clarity, and clarity leads to wisdom. Clarity and wisdom will always lead you to your truth! Living your authentic truth will always magnetize the perfect people to you, thus, always leading to the ideal relationships for that particular moment in time.

The problem with most of us is that we have been searching for "Mr. or Ms. Right" for so long, that we interpret situations inaccurately. The reason we do this is usually because we feel *desperate*. The only reason we feel desperate is because of what we were taught. Our *beliefs* can take us down a destructive path, which can turn into a vicious cycle. This cycle seems to continue generation after generation riddled with misinterpretation or brainwashing!

In this *Information Age* where we can literally connect with the entire world in a matter of seconds, you can see how personalities would be more diversified than ever before. You can also imagine how it would be difficult to communicate without a few disagreements or arguments given the billions of possibilities and different points of view that take place every moment of every day. With this kind of equation, how could anyone even remotely think identically or without differences?

If we want our relationships to be optimal, then we must *consciously* take care of ourselves. This means taking responsibility without *selling out*, continuously listening to our inner voice, and staying, remaining and *living in the moment*. We must consciously go with our instincts and intuition... rather than our mind. Every step we take must be genuine and authentic. This will enable us to always be the best we can possibly be. Living a lie takes too much effort.

Love is probably different for everyone, but anything over and above what I've already mentioned is icing on the cake! When you feel that you just *can't* come from a loving heart, then stay home and look in the mirror naked. You will know in an instant what you *haven't* been giving yourself. Whenever your needs *aren't* met, it may be a challenge to come from kindness and generosity. That's why you must treat yourself as if you were already a prince or princess and deserving of everything good.

If you have temporarily *forgotten* who you are, then immediately go and do some deep, conscious breathing through your nose and out through your mouth for a few minutes, until you reach the "alpha" state of mind. Remember to write down your thoughts. This helps to release any *toxic thoughts* as well as discharge physical obstructions.

It's true that we don't need to please the world, but we do need to treat others as we wish to be treated. Always remember *not* to throw your pearls before swine. I've had to learn to walk away from selfish, ignorant, destructive, negative, individuals.

Most people refuse to change until they *have to,* or until *they're ready…*and not a second sooner! We use whatever methods or lessons are available to us at any given moment. Unfortunately, most of us need to hurt *very* badly before we make the necessary changes. To find peace, and make our own way in life, we all seem to take different roads to reach the same final destination! Some of us just have more restricted thinking than others have. This is why we should be with someone for at least a year before committing for life. More often than not, a person's narrow-mindedness just doesn't always show up until it's too late.

I love mankind, it's just that I finally realized that it's not my job to change or fix the world. I had to stop trying to play God to find inner peace. In writing this book, I get to write about my experiences along with the points of views that now appear to be my truth at this time and phase of life.

I don't profess to have all of the answers. But I sure have found a lot of peace in my heart. I wake up happy everyday. I'm so grateful for what I already have. I no longer compare myself to others. I now love who I see in the mirrored reflection. I don't know too many people who can honestly say that. I *feel* blessed, and I am grateful, regardless of the *circumstances*.

If I can offer my *roadmap*, which is this book *and* my CD, to anyone who feels the calling to read, and/or listen to it, *and it assists them*...then I *know* this journey was all worth it. If I can make a difference in even a single life by effectively pointing out the roads that were bumpy along the way, and give you directions for the alternate path, and it changes the course of your life for the better, then I'm happy.

I just don't believe that any one person can ever fit every single *picture* we have of an ideal mate. Relationships are all give and take, and if you feel that yours has been off balance, then I'm suggesting that you take a good look at the price you've been paying, and ask yourself...is it worth it?

Have you sold your own soul by throwing your pearls to unworthy swine? If you continue to do so, you'll have no pearls left to give! You now know that if you've been doing that...*you need to stop*!

Sometimes I wonder if our creator ever really intended for humans to spend their lives monogamously, or if we're just here to learn a lot of different lessons from many different people. I certainly don't profess to have all the answers, but maybe our unique and diverse upbringings in life didn't wire us up for that type of one on one, forever...'til death do us part type of situation. Sometimes starting out fresh and on our own sounds like a lot of work, so we continue to *put up with* the nonsense that *is* our current situation.

I believe that *one of the sources of conflicts in relationships* is to shut down and *not* communicate when your mate has just crossed over the *threshold of limitations* that you've set for yourself. Have you been suppressing that piece of vital information to *keep the peace* between you and your mate? I hope not, because you'll have no peace if you don't speak your truth.

What stipulations and terms of your "heart contract" with your inner-child have been unspoken thus far to your mate, spouse or significant other? You become the villain when you sell yourself

122

out. When you speak your truth, and your life partner truly gets it...they know never to cross over that line again. They wouldn't even think of hurting or abusing you in any way once they become empathetically educated and liberated from their unconsciousness and ignorance.

I heard the phrase "emotional safety" mentioned recently. We've all set up *barriers* of one form or another throughout our lives. We think we're using these barriers to protect ourselves during vulnerable moments in life to feel more secure. I believe if we pay attention by observing and listening, that we won't need any barriers, and that our faith, natural knowing, responsible communication, and trust will eliminate the need for *any* safety nets, other than physical ones. The more you love and nurture yourself, the quicker you can dissolve and unleash the invisible chains that have kept you in bondage for far too long, so that you never need to *hide* behind anything ever again.

What attracts or entices people to you? Is it chemistry, science, *or* even voodoo? Is it your charm or finesse? Is it your appearance or mannerisms that determine whether someone is repelled by you, or drawn to you? Is our *belief system* or what we were taught so powerful, that we *do* chemically entice or lure the perfect mate? If everything *is* mind over matter, and we can really change our thoughts and beliefs, then maybe we can change our chemistry, and attract people who embrace our energy for *who* and *what* we already are...in our natural state, without pretense.

Imagine everyone in the world being in relationships without *ever* having or trying to convince, contrive, maneuver, or manipulate anyone into loving us. But rather, that our own love for ourselves *is* the attraction.

When we pay attention, we will always *recognize the signs* that provide insight as to when it's time to let go, release, and disengage from people. When you feel like you're constantly being backed into a corner...that's usually pretty good evidence of something not working. If you know you've responsibly tried everything from complete honest communication, to counseling, to separation, but ultimately you're at an impasse and your differences are irreconcilable, then acknowledge the growth and lessons you've shared with one another, and move on. This is your life! Don't get stuck by living in the past or by hoping and wishing for what could have been. The creator may simply have a different plan for you.

If you're being taken for granted and are unappreciated by your loved ones, that should not be tolerated. Why would you or anyone else want to hold on to something, not only knowing it doesn't work, but also knowing clearly that it's destructive and a waste of your precious time! Remember...we always know when it's time to move on. Sometimes it seems so hard and even terrifying but through the forest and the trees, the light will pull you out if you allow yourself to stay focused. We don't need to wait until so much anger sets in that we actually begin *hating* our mate.

To stay in certain situations is not only crippling; it's actually a disservice to everyone around you, because you just can't play full out. Once you finally create the courage to walk away, the "abusive partner" usually wants you back. This is because they had the opportunity to finally miss you and appreciate *what they "had"*, and see the errors of their ways. (Or, it's a matter of "control" over you and they want it back.) But it's frequently too late because the damage has been done. Depending on the level of maturity and the strength of the foundation you previously built together will determine if your relationship can withstand the test of time. It's very unfortunate that most people never realize what they had until they've lost it. We tend to take so much for granted in life.

It's true that none of us know what's going to happen from one moment to the next. We can make all kinds of plans, but there are just too many external forces to try to *control* anything. If you want to make God laugh...tell *her* your plans! The best thing you can do is be responsible when making changes that affect other people. Also, be sure that you feel *centered, balanced,* and *reasonable* before you make *any* final decisions or choices.

After The Sex Is Over:

Does your life feel *worth living* when you're around someone in particular? If it does and continues to blossom after a year, then "grab that person up and marry them!" I'm not talking about a sexual encounter here. That's another book entirely. I'm talking about after the sex is over, how are you working out on an intellectual level? After all, there are many forms of intimacy.

What's the level of friendship you both experience when you spend time together? In other words, what's the *quality* of your relationship? My mate and I have made a conscious choice to stay and work out each day's new challenges. When it's all said and done...we like each other!

We all need to be flexible and open minded enough to adapt and adjust to ever changing situations so that life feels worth living with *and* without a life partner. I constantly have to RE-CHOOSE along the way. But if I can change certain situations to suit my needs...I will. I always keep my integrity intact if I want to *like* that which I see in the mirror.

Sometimes our *judgment seems impaired* because of what appears to be "heavy burdens." It's at times like these, that our life choices may not be wise or well thought out. This is when deep conscious breathing is more important than ever before. The circulation of oxygen to your brain, created by this conscious breathing will assist you in not wasting precious time by worrying. Since you can't *buy* time, why would you ever want to waste any?

Imagine living the life you love.
Imagine waking up on a daily basis
With a smile on your face!

If you're not loving the life you live, and living the life you love, you'll want to read this book again and again until you're inclined to wake up *wearing a smile* and being grateful for everything you have. It's just too painful and takes too much time to personally experience and grow from the many lessons that we incur, just for being human. If I had paid more attention, I know I would have been spared a lot of heartache, suffering, and struggle. So read on...maybe you'll get *what I didn't* so long ago. Remember...knowing what you *don't* want is half the battle! Here's a portion of an email I just received:

Marry a person you love to talk to.
As you get older, their conversational skills
Will be as important as any other.
When you say, *"I love you,"* mean it.
When you say, *"I'm sorry,"* look the person in the eye.

Love deeply and passionately.
You might get hurt but it's the only way to live life completely.
In disagreements, fight fairly...No name-calling.

Talk slowly but think quickly.
Remember that great love and great achievements
Involve great risk.
When you lose, don't lose the lesson.

Remember the *Three R's:*
Respect for self
Respect for others
Be responsible for all your actions.

Don't let a little dispute injure a great friendship.
When you realize you've made a mistake,
take immediate steps to correct it.
Spend some time alone.

The MYTH about Oxygen and Exercise
...What you "don't know" can make you FAT!

> "The care of the 'part' should not be attempted
> without treatment of the 'whole'"
> – Plato

This chapter will help you attain clarity and understanding about *how* the body works so that you can create *and* maintain the optimally healthy body of *your* dreams!

You'll never have weight challenges once you understand how the human anatomy works. To make sense of this very important chapter I had to really look at the human anatomy as not only *a science of living organisms*, but also as an assemblage of *thoughts, feelings,* and *beliefs*. It would all be so easy, if we could just say "take charge, exercise, and eat less!" Life just isn't that simple however. The fact is...we are so much more complex...especially because we have a *mind*. We're dealing with an imbedded irrational and illogical collective consciousness of universal thoughts, as well as imbalance of our chemistry, and a body of laws and principles to deal with. You must allow your mind to reverse or release these senseless thoughts.

We'll delve into the management of our thoughts in the final chapter on affirmations, but for now, let's learn how to release the residue that's been holding us back and plaguing us for far too long.

It may *appear* as if *circumstances in the environment* brought about the disease, the excess fat, *and even* the immense debts that you currently owe to society. Once you begin to address all of the circumstantial *issues* and *challenges* that occur on a daily basis however, everything in your life will start to change, simply because you took charge *and* just because *you say so*. We will never again be able to blame anyone for the way our life turned out. Since we know there are always consequences when we *suppress* our concerns...why not just deal with each issue as it occurs?

There are specific actions, or things you can do to accelerate your healing process. This entire book has been dedicated to your healing from the inside out…but also, to find as much comfort as humanly possible while *residing* in your skin.

Isn't it now time to finally liberate yourself from the immense stack of burdens you have been using to poison your body, mind, and spirit with for so very long? Isn't it now time to take a stand and take charge of all areas of your life? By allowing yourself to address each dissatisfying issue, your *excess baggage* will begin to dissolve on a daily basis, which will *include* your excess fat.

The more quality time you give yourself, the more quickly the *junk* in your life will disappear. The shackles of debt, obesity, illness, fear, and depression that have held you in captivity will diminish and eventually fall away. How much longer are you willing to drag around this heavy cargo? You deserve better!

Most people, who withhold *or* suppress communication, begin to feel like something is eating at them, whether it's males, who were taught as young boys to be tough and macho, or females who were taught, you're not good enough!

This type of restraint ultimately brings about many unsatisfying situations and conditions in people's lives. For now however, we'll just discuss the issue *of overeating*, which leads to substituting food *for* comfort, rather than just addressing these issues directly as they occur. In such cases, the appetite becomes so uncontrollable that they end up using food as a pacifier. For some people…this could go on for years, then, one day, they wish to lose weight, but can't seem to do so, because something seems to be *eating at them*. It's all about suppressing their emotions or *undelivered communication*. They're either lying to themselves or others, and the only way to find honest answers is to go deep within, and finally just *deal with it* all! In doing this, their self-image will be altered by having a more wholesome and positive state of mind.

Our habits can be changed whenever we decide to take *the leap into faith*, which can only come from *already having* faith. You can see how this vicious cycle could persist, until we decide to change our thoughts, patterns, and habits. Remember…*faith* and *fear* cannot live in the same place at the same time.

128

We pay a serious price every time we ignore communication that needs to be expressed. When you begin to communicate in a responsible way, you grow and mature. With this growth, you'll become more balanced, wise, and more clear than ever before in your life. This will aid you in designing and sculpting your ideal body, but there's still so much more *work* to be done.

We always need to remember that it took us a lifetime to get our bodies into the appearance *and* state they're currently in. We need to be patient and allow time for any changes that will ultimately occur...*to happen gradually.* One new piece of information can drastically change our life forever. Just *how much* you really want something will *show up* "in your new body" and "your new attitude," because we know that talk is cheap! Your *actions* will eventually speak volumes. The little "mini-you" is just hanging out and waiting for you to see the light. Before long you *will* feel comfortable in your own skin.

We always need to *allow time* to process and integrate all the new information that comes our way. Growth takes time, and there's no need to rush the process. This is why it's important not to ever throw yourself into something without thinking it all the way through first. It's easy to get confused when trying to differentiate old beliefs and habits from new ones, but over time, as you process new information that comes your way, it will all begin to make sense. Before long, you will feel comfort in your own skin on a daily basis. You will wake up happy every day merely because *you took charge.*

If it's true we only have excuses, reasons, *or* results in our lives, then we need to take a look at *what* has been holding us back from having what we want. As you look at your life right now, what do you see? Is everything running smoothly like a fine-tuned machine? Are you happy? Are you living the life you love? Are you living the life you envisioned as an adolescent? If not, why not? Are you getting results *by design* or simply settling for the way things fall? What *beliefs, reasons* and *excuses* are you using to keep yourself stuck in old patterns and habits?

<u>We need to stop comparing</u>! Things are rarely ever what they appear to be! Before I worked at the Nordstrom Dept. Store many years

ago, I used to think that almost everyone had a *perfect body*...except me. When I worked with many women in the dressing rooms, I was quick to realize that every one of them wanted or needed to change some aspect of their image. Too tall, too short, too fat, too thin, too ugly, no confidence, no self-esteem, no this, no that, too this, too that! I noticed that everyone wanted to look like someone else. There's just no satisfaction in that!

Just because someone appears to look a certain way doesn't mean they're happy or sad; positive or negative; healthy or ridden with disease. Looks are so deceiving, and the grass is *not* always greener on the other side! It's all *what we* make of it! We see "model-like" physically beautiful people everywhere. We see couples who appear to be happy...but they don't even like each other when they're home alone together. Don't be fooled by appearances or what you *think* you see!

Taking the necessary steps: If you're going to live another day on this planet, don't you want to feel, look, and live optimally in true health, love, joy, prosperity, clarity, wisdom, confidence, and enthusiasm? The first question is... *"Are you willing to now have it all?"* And... *"Just 'how good' are you willing to have it?"*

Let's take the first steps by adjusting and adapting to new breathing techniques, but before we do...I have **only one rule**...every morning when you wake up, before you even put your feet on the ground...immediately put your feet into your *walking or work-out shoes*. Don't even let your feet touch the ground. The reason is so that you can *move* your way to a more healthy body. **This pair of shoes will become your best friend!** Putting on these magical shoes will set you up to win! Once they're on your feet, if you then choose *not* to exercise, that's completely up to you. However, you're already half way home, so you may as well *at least* take a morning walk...**just do it!** When I put on my shoes...I become *ready for action!*

No matter where you are in life, always be *consciously* breathing...not just taking in shallow tidbits of air. Take long deep breaths. It's proven that the clearest thinking occurs when a flow of oxygen infiltrates our bodily cells and brain. Continuous deep breathing brings about a wonderful precise clarity that can take you closer to Nirvana, heaven, and your creator than just about anything on the planet.

The leaner you are, the more deeply you can breathe, because there is less obstruction. Obstruction represents past and present tensions, entanglements, and complications in your life. This deep conscious breathing will ultimately take you to the essence of your *inner core*. After all, information does seem to flow more easily in an open vessel. Keep the breathing going, for this type of deep conscious breathing creates heat and circulation, which burns fat. The oxygen actually burns into the fat, until ultimately, it begins to dissolve and disappear. One day, you look into the mirror and see the new, thinner *you* emerge.

The benefits of conscious breathing are so vast. I could write volumes on this topic alone. I've trained my body over the past few years to *remember* to breathe deeply. Breathing deeply activates the metabolism and also dissolves negative thoughts. Over time, you'll notice that you're naturally eating smaller meals throughout each and every day from this point forward. Your body just no longer has the need or desire to overeat. The types of foods you put in will *very much determine* the way you'll feel each and every day. In the next chapter, I'll speak a lot about what *different types* of foods do, *and* how they make you *feel.*

This method of continuous conscious breathing will put you in an alpha state of mind. This process is life altering! A transformation will occur throughout your entire body. You will experience yourself thinking more clearly, as you reach this meditative and contemplative composed condition. It's as if you actually feel the demons disappear and unleash themselves, as the new, real, "*loving you*" comes out to play. The more you breathe, ultimately the leaner and more focused you will become. These benefits *alone* are substantial enough to have anyone continue this process, no matter how lazy you may have felt *before* reading this book. I'll describe *how* to breathe in more depth later in this chapter.

Over time this deep breathing will make you more aware of your true heart's desire, and will aid in promoting the dissolution of the excess fat that has plagued you for so very long. *Speak to your fat*, as you stretch and breathe into it. Thank your excess fat for it's protection throughout the years. Let it know that you are ready to move on with your life, and that it has served you well, but that it's protective services are just no longer needed. Affirm the following..."I now lovingly and consciously release my excess fat!" Learn to face the world again without wearing a shield of lard. Come out to play again at the game of life and show your *authentic self.*

As you speak to your fat, thank it for *already being gone*. Watch it disappear from your outer extremities *first*. Think about it. Excess weight first shows up in our mid-section, around our belly. Then the weight clings and grows *outward*, away from the stomach region to the entire trunk of our body...into our arms, neck, and face. The same downward spiral occurs from the abdominal area down toward our buns, thighs, calves, and ankles. So it only stands to reason that we would *release weight* beginning with the face, neck, and then arms downward into the trunk, *and* from the ankles, calves, thighs, and buns upward.

The bottom line is the first place to gain weight is the abdomen, and the last place to release weight is the abdomen. This would make our mid-section *appear* larger than life if we were to *focus* on that area alone. It seems to be human nature to zoom in on the areas that look most unappealing, which gives us a distorted view of ourselves. You would never just zoom in on your best friend's abdominal area and hate them for having a large belly. So stop being so mean to your self.

As you begin to *really* look in the mirror...start to see what's *good* about you, and stay focused on that. Lovingly allow the excess weight to dissolve and release itself. If it's any consolation, since well over 50% of our population are obese, you're not alone. Knowing this should make it easier for you to forgive yourself for abusing or neglecting your body, since you're simply part of the majority. Once you forgive yourself, you're more than halfway home in attaining everything you want in life. Remember to *be careful what you ask for* as you go through life.

A few months ago, I created a very effective process that only takes 1 to 3 minutes. Whenever I do this process, I feel as if a laser literally enters my brain and burns out any *negative accumulated thoughts*. I call the process "defrag."

When you defragment a computer...a *grid* of tiny box-like shapes will appear on the computer screen. The purpose of defragmenting is to remove debris and scattered information from your computer. Every area of the grid is actually scanned thoroughly until each hindrance or interference is gone. Then it's aligned so it can function faster and more efficiently.

Here's how you "defrag" your *mental interference*. Go outside, sit in a chair, close your eyes ever so gently and face the sun. In your mind's eye you'll see a bright, red-hot screen that appears to have tiny grids. You *must* face the sun, so be sure to have your eyes closed! Allow your eyes to *flutter* while they're closed ever so gently. This fluttering is very much like REM or rapid eye movement that takes place during the dream process. In your mind's eye, this will create a rippling effect, which will give the appearance of the tiny grids defragmenting...just like on a computer.

It will appear as if a continuous current is drifting along, row by row, from the top left corner of your mind, flitting along to the right, and then back again. (Like a typewriter keyboard in constant use.) This continuous flashing and flowing will begin to make you feel like you're in a trance. All confusion, disarray, and clutter that plagued your mind will feel like the heat of the sun is electrically removing it. You'll almost immediately feel yourself become *centered, recharged* and *revitalized.*

Since we *know* how vital oxygen is, we must also *understand* the importance of water. Quenching your thirst *constantly* will keep your cells and organs hydrated so they can perform and function properly. Unpolluted, uncontaminated, clean, filtered, pure water is like sharing nectar with the Gods. I don't go *anywhere* without carrying a bottle of clean drinking water. The more you drink, the more it will aid in purifying, detoxifying, and relieving you of hidden toxins. *Prevention* is key in taking responsibility for your health and well-being.

Unfortunately, most people *assume* they get sick because of genetic predisposition and that it's their fate. I'm sure you've heard people tell themselves, and believe without question, that they "...have arthritis because my mother did" or they "...have diabetes because their grandparents did," and so on. Even though genetics *obviously* plays an important role, these people have already verbally condemned themselves into actually generating poor health.

In fact, making a few intelligent choices and incorporating them into one's life can *prevent* most diseases. Even if you've already been diagnosed with a disease, begin to turn your habits and negative thinking around *now* and reverse the process before it goes any further.

Toxins get stuck in the deep crevices of our excess fat, our organs, and every other part of our body. We must learn how to release these poisons and impurities *before* they do damage. One of the ways we can reverse the disease and aging process is to understand the term "free radical." "Free radicals" create oxidative damage inside our bodies and destroy the integrity and healthy functioning of our cells. They are simply unpaired electrons that seek a "mate" inside our body.

Here is an example of how the effects of "free radical damage" appear to the naked eye. I'm sure you've noticed that after peeling a banana or cutting open an apple it begins to turn brown almost immediately. The reason for this discoloration is because oxygen damages the integrity of cells. However, if you were to immediately apply lemon juice, they wouldn't turn brown. Why? Because the lemon provides vitamin C which protects the cells from oxidative damage and destruction.

There are many different anti-oxidants we can use to supplement our diet. I wish this was all we ever needed to do, but it's not. Since these free radicals literally undermine and destroy our healthy cells, it is absolutely essential that we take the necessary precautions to preserve our health. Unfortunately, free radicals have no prejudice. *They attack everyone* on a daily basis, and you're no exception. The question then becomes... *"How do we combat the free radicals?"*

134

This is where supplementation is so vitally necessary, but not with just any ol' product.

As a result of having done extensive research over the past 30 years, my partner and I have chosen USANA *Health Sciences* as our health supplements supplier. Their facility is FDA approved, which by law means that what's on the label *must* match the ingredients. Most vitamin suppliers *and* manufacturers do *not* have *FDA* approved facilities which means by law, they need to contain only 20% of what's listed on the panel. This is absurd and potentially hazardous to your health! Can you imagine thinking you're purchasing a product with specific proportions and you may only be getting 20% of what is actually listed? How can we knowingly trust any supplements that are sold in the stores? Most products are just not worth the cost of their packaging.

We've been taking the entire Usana product line religiously since 1994 and would never knowingly miss a day. I attribute much of my health and well-being to these amazing products. The Founder and Chairman of *USANA*, Dr. Myron Wentz, founded *Gull Laboratories* in 1974 where he set the "Gold Standard" for developing viral disease diagnostic tests followed worldwide since the early '70s. At *Gull Labs,* Dr. Wentz developed over 30 viral disease tests for such viruses as the *Epstein-Barr virus,* and such diseases as *Hepatitis A & B, Herpes I & II, Mononucleosis, etc.*

Dr. Wentz has grown upwards of 40 billion human cells every day for over 20 years keeping them completely healthy and disease free. *These cells are as healthy today as they were 20 years ago* because of Dr. Wentz' unparalleled understanding of cellular nutrition. In other words, he and his international team of scientists, physicians, and other health professionals know what the body needs to be perfectly balanced and healthy.

Knowing Dr. Wentz personally, I know through experience that he is not only a man who truly cares about assisting people in having optimal health, he takes no shortcuts. I would never trust my health to the lowest bidder! In fact, in order to assure the highest quality, you cannot purchase Usana products in stores, and also Dr. Wentz knew the importance of people sharing their experience through word of mouth. I've put my health and well-being in the hands of the caring people at *USANA Health Sciences.*

By the way, *Sensé* (pronounced "Sahn-Say") - which is *USANA's* anti-aging skin care line is unsurpassed as are its Lean Weight Management and Life Long Health products. Since the skin is the largest organ of the body, we must be particularly careful about the products we apply. Usana's products are next generation science!

If anyone has ever approached you about this product, I would suggest you call him or her immediately and tell them you wish to order and automatically receive this product every month. If no one has approached you, either leave a message on the voice mail number 800-567-3602. Or, call Lori Bell direct at 801-954-7203. Mention J'en El referred you and you will be well taken care of. You can also go to **www.FindingComfort.com** for more details..

It's amazing that doctors are the first to admit that their nutritional education was minimal. The average student of nutrition knows more about the topic than doctors do. I have the utmost respect for MDs, as I have many uncles, cousins, friends and a brother who are doctors. Overall, their *nutritional* education is simply not adequate. Our soil has become so depleted over time that our foods just *can't* give us what we need to maintain a healthy, balanced body. If you hear anyone say…*"You can get all of your nutritional needs met from your foods,"* I would suggest that you RUN…and Run fast!

As intricate as the human body is, it tends to adapt itself to most of the abuse and bad habits one has cultivated throughout one's life. The body gradually and methodically responds and adapts until one day, it just can't take any more abuse and it starts to break down in many different ways. Ultimately, diseases catch up with most of us before long. If we don't quickly learn to discern the difference between healthy vs. diseased, then a quick dose of reality is sure to show up in the form of cancer, stroke, heart failure, diabetes, etc. Hopefully *before* that happens, you'll begin to eagerly make enthusiastic and passionate changes.

One of the kindest things you can do for yourself is to be gentle, loving, and kind to your best friend in the world…that would be you! If you persevere in the right direction, your body will have no choice but to respond to your loving commands over time. You're so worth the best!

Regardless of the dual role that oxygen plays, we need to understand how to combat oxidative damage to our cells, as well as always remember the important role that conscious breathing plays in aiding with the elimination of cloudy and negative thoughts. Negative thoughts could otherwise impair our inner-visions.

Getting oxygen to the brain helps us think more lucidly. This clarity of thought will enable you to *reconstruct your life* in a rational, sensible and logical manner. Remember, one of the keys to staying clear throughout life, is to write down the things that come up during your meditation and breathing exercises. This is just taking care of business, which is ultimately, really *taking care of you*.

Your new insights will enable you to replace the old negative thoughts with updated positive ideas, which will allow you to take control of your life and finally have everything the way you want...especially a beautiful, lean, healthy body. The suffering will gradually diminish and disappear if you address each issue as it arises.

Imagine creating, arranging, and designing your life...as a composer would, to a sheet of music. Taking charge in this way will allow you the freedom to finally reside in your own perfect body, and metamorphose into the beautiful, free butterfly that awaits to emerge deep from within. The more deeply we breath, and the more water we drink, the more cleansed we can become. I would never go anywhere without my water. Life and health depend on it.

There are many different ways to breathe properly, but the most basic and helpful is to inhale slowly and deeply *in* through your nose. When you've taken in all you can, hold your breath for a few moments until you feel the urge to naturally release slowly and smoothly through your mouth. Toxins will be released with each breath that is discharged. The more you do this, the more euphoric, exhilarating, stimulating, invigorating, enlivening, happy, joyful, and elated you'll begin to feel. Drinking water and remembering to consciously breathe will add a new dimension of joy that will enable you to feel more and more comfortable in your skin for as long as you live.

ACTION STEP #2 - *Enhance* your life by beginning with the *types* of exercises that **you** enjoy. Routines can become "ruts" without even trying. Be open to *change*, and the world will disclose itself to you in beautiful new ways. You can be creative and turn almost anything into a fun time while renovating and rejuvenating your body, mind, and soul.

If you're sitting at the computer, you can breathe and squeeze your buns. You can take long walks and listen to affirmations using your Sony Walkman. By listening to your favorite music as you breathe and walk, make sure you pay attention to the green of nature that surrounds you and breathe that in! These natural surroundings will bring you a high source of energy. Even when you make love, you must breathe deeply from the core in order to have a really satisfying orgasm.

We already know that we either have excuses *or* results in our life, so why not choose *results*? I used to make up every excuse in the book as to why I couldn't exercise. Not enough time or I was too tired were the ones I used the most. Now, I've learned that I *must* make the time to exercise, and you know what…everything I need to get done, always gets done anyway, because oxygen and muscle strength make you feel more energized and motivated. It's a vicious cycle to get caught up in *arguing* why you *can't* do something. JUST DO IT!

Take one day at a time and *then* see what happens. Give yourself a *minimum* of 12 weeks of diligently going through the recommendations I mention throughout this book. If, after this 3-month period, you wish to stop, give yourself permission to do that. You probably won't want to stop once you see *and* feel the subtle changes that will have occurred throughout your body *and* because you've already replaced your old habits with new ones. Don't expect miracles right away. Just know that a gorgeous, vibrant, curvaceous, or buff physique is waiting inside to be released. After all, the circulation alone will give your appearance a healthier glow.

138

Once you start working out with weights long enough to reverse atrophy or shrinking of your muscles, the closer you'll be to having a more satisfying appearance to your body. No one likes the effects of *gravity* on the human body. If you want to preserve your health, you'll have to start sooner or later, so why not now...today! Oprah says "Work out with weights and fight for everything you get!" She's right on accurate. Quite honestly; I don't like the way osteoporosis *or* flab looks on a human being, not to mention the danger of having weak bones or uncomfortable back problems that usually occur with excess body mass.

Take your actions one step further and buy a Polaroid camera. Since people love to *see* results... take a picture once or twice a week and write the date on the back of each photo. Put them in a place where only you can see the gradual results week after week, month after month, until you've attained your desired results. Over time, that will actually *show you the effects* produced by eating better foods, because on the back of each photo, you're going to write down *everything* you put in your body on a daily basis. This is playing "Show and Tell" with your self. Looking in the mirror and taking Polaroid's will also assist you in *designing your* perfect body. I will discuss various options of *conscious eating* in the next chapter.

At the age of 30, I stopped exercising. I specifically remember the reasons that I used to give up "my then beautiful body." I used the excuse that men just liked me because my body looked sexy. The transformation I allowed to occur to my figure over the next 18 years of a sedentary lifestyle brought a new meaning to the words gravity and atrophy. I gained 30+ pounds that *did not* look appealing on my 5' frame. I started to wear dresses that looked like *"mumus."* You know the ones...they make you look like a shopping bag with two legs and a head!

In my late 40's, I regained my sanity and joined a gym. I hired a personal trainer for 8 to 10 sessions *only,* so that I could learn *the basics* all over again. I was such a wimp at first. I started out *really* slow. Gradually, I breathed into each movement until it began to feel good. Adding heavier weights began to turn my old, dilapidated, flabby body into a leaner more defined one. It was a miracle. It took longer than I wanted, but what's the hurry? As long as the path is consistently upward, that was all that mattered. Of course there are days when I temporarily fall back into old habits and eat foods that don't serve me. (Fatty, salty, greasy...crap.) But that's always *my conscious choice.* That's where the magic is...*choice.* These days, more often than not, I *choose* to eat healthy foods. I feel more vibrant and productive when I do. Finally my new choices are second nature *and* show up as my primary habit.

As boredom began to set in, I knew I had to have alternatives, instead of a routine, so I've learned how to *diversify my exercises* in order to keep it fun. Also...different exercises make you move different parts of your body. Some exercises make you breathe harder, yet other movements break down fat more quickly. Weight and resistance exercises build muscle. They're all good. Do whatever makes you feel great, as often as possible, but never lose the momentum! It's too hard when you have to keep starting all over again

Since I love being in the privacy of my own home, I customized a tiny area of my bedroom to accommodate my needs. I purchased a few pieces of basic equipment at *Wal-Mart.* (I love that store...you can get just about anything you need there.) A few sets of inexpensive weights, and a *Sony Walkman* to go along with the *work-out shoes,* and you've set your self up to win.

I even joined *Time-Life Music* and ordered dozens of my favorite classics in CD format so I can dance, stretch, and workout to whatever music I'm in the mood for at any given moment. I play many different types of music to create *specific* outcomes. Sometimes, I'm in the mood for slow, methodical movements. Sometimes, faster, and more deliberate moves feel better. Now and then, we all just need a day off. As long as you're consistently moving <u>at least</u> 3 to 5 times per week, you're ahead of the game. Remember that it takes a good 20 minutes to get your heartbeat and pulse to a higher rate, which is when the benefits start to occur.

When I do aerobics, I purposefully play my old disco tunes. When I wish to do yoga, stretching, isometrics or meditation, I intentionally choose a soothing piece of music. Music creates different moods, so tune-in to your inner voice and listen to find out what your body is in the mood for that day. Some days I'll put on a fast tune, but my body just won't respond. Then I'll put on something more peaceful to do isometrics with weights and just sort of hang in different positions, so that different muscle groups benefit. Some days I like to go to the gym and lift weights and workout on the heavy equipment that provide resistance.

On other days I just like to stay home and work out to old videos I purchased over the years, which feature a variety of exercises, such as aerobics, Pilates, Yoga, Callinetics, Jane Fonda, boxing, Buns & Abs of Steel. Sometimes riding a bike, jogging or walking briskly is the way to go. They're all good! Sometimes I just like to sit in front of the television and *do nothing*! It's all about paying attention to the way you feel and giving *you* permission to do what you need as often as possible. This is freedom in its truest form! It also keeps you out of a "rut."

I found it very helpful to exercise without clothing. Look in the mirror naked while dancing or moving and *consciously* breathe deeply to your favorite music. (Yes...it's a sight to behold!) When I first began dancing naked, I felt embarrassed. Later, I felt ashamed for not taking better care of myself for so many years. Disco, however, really made me *want* to move. I started breathing into the fatty areas, actually *willing, sculpting,* and *breathing* my body back into shape.

I had to face the fact that the mirror doesn't lie, so I began to *speak* to my fat as I breathed deeply into those areas that seemed to have a will of their own. Sometimes I wondered if the excess fat would linger forever. That's when I remembered an old trick I learned in the early 80's. I began to use 100 mg of niacin (Vitamin B3), and then increased my dosage up to 500 mg over time.

Niacin improves circulation and increases blood flow. The downfall is that it doesn't smell very good to some people, so I only take it before workouts. I actually see a red flush throughout my body from my head to my toes, as well as a feeling of heat burning through the fat inside of my cells. It's really amazing. Keep in mind that the "flush" will diminish or disappear entirely if the niacin is taken everyday, so use it sparingly. Also...the effect is not as strong if taken with food.

It was at this point in time that I became *very conscious* of my food intake. I realized that if I stopped putting in the wrong fatty foods, and started replacing my meals with conscious, delicious, natural foods, that one day, the old rancid fat would have no other alternative but to literally dissolve away. I was about to *define* myself not only with muscle, but *who* I was about to become. I was also about to *determine my boundaries* as a human being.

I began to read extensively and study the *effects* that different foods have on the body. Religiously experimenting until one day, I looked into the mirror naked, and actually started to see a lean body with a hint of definition emerging from underneath a protected padding of insulated excess fat that had shielded me from the world for so very long. The sight of curves, definition, and muscle not only delighted me, but also renewed my faith. I became more determined than ever to have what was rightfully mine...the lean body that God had originally blessed me with so many years ago. The mere *possibilities* brought tears of gratitude and joy to my eyes.

In diversifying your exercise regime, you will strengthen a wide variety of the many muscles distributed, throughout your body. REMEMBER to enjoy and *be aware* during each breath *and* each movement. Don't ever *watch the clock* dreading what you're doing or having the thoughts of "I hate this," or "it hurts."

Just be in the moment and pay attention to each breath and really *feel* the contributions that these moves are making to your body. Prolong each movement, as if your body loves you for giving it the attention it deserves...because it does! This will make the process enjoyable *and* self-reinforcing. This is where looking in the mirror while naked *really* makes the most sense. This is where speaking to your fat also makes a lot of sense. Love your fat away.

Alternating muscle groups on different days works very well. This way you won't burn out, and you'll give your muscles time to heal and adjust to the new healthy you. Your body needs attention, and until you decide to give it...you're diminishing your capacity for true health. It's okay to be sedentary *at times*! Everything in life should be done within reason. If you haven't exercised for years...be responsible and start slowly! Be GENTLE with yourself and push a *little* beyond your comfort level...gradually, until you know you've taken charge of your body. Always keep checking in with yourself! At first, your body may hurt, but if you gently and deliberately persist...you'll win! If there's pain, know that it's temporary! Your minimal *pain* will turn into a successive *gain*.

If you remain consistent, your body will adapt to this new way of life and you will start to feel better. Later on, you will begin to feel great. As you persist, you might even get upset if you have to miss an exercise session...due to unforeseen circumstances. There's nothing in the world quite like exercise. It's the *attitude* we have about exercise that has kept us from it for so long. It stimulates and circulates which really lets you know you're alive. Even your eyesight may improve.

The definition of exercise is action, use, perform, apply, play, fun, recreation, sport, movement, and energy. Knowing that everything will start to function better if you persist, I know you'll be able to come up with some forms of movement that make you feel good, and that you can enjoy. Just Do It!

As you see from these definitions, each word leads to something better. I promise there will be a rainbow on the other side of any temporary discomfort. Once you begin...never stop! Make it a habit. Make it a way of life! The benefits are vast. People who exercise regularly seem to have a natural glow as opposed to people who remain sedentary.

Just remember that Rome wasn't built in a day. You may not see or feel *any* results for weeks *or* even months. That's okay. After all, what's the rush? If you have NO EXPECTATIONS, then you can never be disappointed. Eventually, you *will* see and feel results. Remember that it took us a lifetime to get our body to the condition it's in. What matters is that you start *now* and know that the results you've been dreaming about will happen. You're worth the time that it takes!

As time passes by, you'll actually see your muscles and skin respond by redistributing themselves. Your skin will appear tighter and your muscles will become more defined. It's a beautiful, marvelous and even miraculous sight to behold, when you can finally *see* your physical accomplishments in the mirror *and* in the photos you've taken.

When you can get past the *point of no return* long enough to overpower *your mind* and to give your body *naturally* what it's been lacking for so long, your life will revert to your innate *default state* of happiness. The *formula* is easy...move your body, breathe deeply and consciously, eat nutritiously whenever possible for high energy, and take the highest quality nutritional supplements you can find. If you love yourself, you'll *never* allow yourself to go back to the old ways and habits that didn't serve you for so long.

Go ahead now...give your self everything you've ever wanted. Move that body, floss those teeth, and give yourself facials, manicures, and pedicures. Take charge of your life again.

We Americans have become so lazy and spoiled with ourselves over time. We want everything right now! The truth is, *life is busy,* so we must *make time for ourselves* regardless of circumstances. Abraham Lincoln said, "If I had 8 hours to chop down a tree, I'd spend 6 hours sharpening the ax." I never quite got it until recently. To me, that simply means...*prepare yourself* by putting the necessary time into *you.* This will ultimately give you everything you want throughout your life. Everything is already provided. All we have to do is take the necessary *actions,* in order to receive what's already, legitimately, and rightfully ours.

Move your way to true health and feeling great. Do this *every* day for the rest of your life!

The "Mis"Perception - Food vs. Nutrition
If you knew what I knew, you'd...

> "The doctor of the future will give no medicine,
> but will interest his patients in the care of the human
> frame, diet, and in the prevention of disease."
>
> -Thomas Edison

FOOD, it does a body good...or, does it? It's a well-known fact that if you take in more calories than you burn, you gain weight. So...what most people assume from that, is...they have to eat less. This is nonsense! It's not necessarily *how much* you eat; it's *what* you eat that truly matters. Before we put another morsel of food in our mouths, we should *really understand* the complexity of how *each individual food* affects our body. If you're eating lard/butter/ice cream or any other type of dairy, you're gonna' look like lard. It's a solid mass of fat. It sticks to everything it comes in contact with. Of course it's going to do the same thing *inside* of your body.

It's common sense that when you wash a pan with butter, lard, or oil covering it the only thing that's going to remove it, is soap or detergent. Unfortunately, we can't drink *Joy* dishwashing liquid. So, we must know how to counteract and combat the fat once it's already inside our system.

After many years of research, I learned that specific enzymes synergistically aid in *dissolving fats* that are stored in our bodies. Of course strenuous exercise burns fat, but if you keep putting in as much (or more) fat than you're capable of burning you'll get caught in the vicious frustrating cycle of "*trying*" to lose weight. There's more to understand about this topic, but I'll cover that more specifically in the conscious combining segment, later on.

Don't ever throw yourself into a starvation mode or some fad diet. Learning to eat *consciously* takes time. I believe there are always specific foods to help counteract others. When I feel like my cells are permeated with saturated fat and bloated, it's extremely uncomfortable. So, after consciously breathing (which aids in the digestion process), I wait a few hours and then eat a fruit that is high in natural enzymes, such as pineapple, papaya, mangoes, kiwis, or

145

strawberries. (Be sure to eat each fruit *individually*...not mixed together.) This gives the enzymes contained in each fruit time to perform the way they were designed to. I then go on doing whatever I like to do. The next day I wake up feeling as if I've been naturally cleansed and the fat has been digested and washed out of my body.

The bottom line is this. The more you begin to understand about how food works in your body...the more responsibility you can take *for* your body. I don't care how many books you've already read on this topic. Re-read this chapter many times over. If you pick up even one vital point that you missed along the way (in your past coveting fat life), it could turn your results around immediately. Personally, I wouldn't be willing to risk missing out on *any* piece of *my* puzzle.

As a result of writing this chapter, I got to *re-live* the "maze of fat nightmare" that invaded and plagued my own body for too many years. I hope this information is the key that will assist you in opening the floodgates to *your* happiness and well-being, as it has for me.

Every fat cell that dissolves in your body puts you one step closer to owning your life. Every time we don't like what we see in ourselves, we only need to remember we have choices in *everything* we do. Every choice alters our future. Every step in any given direction affects all of mankind. This makes "thinking things through *beforehand*...very important." Which direction are *you* going?

<u>Losing Weight</u>: The real question is "to carry out *the plan?*" *or* "to sabotage *the plan?*" You get to *make it up* right now, which direction you plan to take. If ultimately, you had no one who really cared about you at the end of each day, the question becomes..."How much does your *final decision* actually matter to *you?*"

Ultimately...it *is* only you *who can* allow yourself to have specific results. No other human on the planet should determine anyone's fate. Why would you ever give that kind of power away to anyone other than yourself? So it's all really about taking *responsibility* for what we each want, as an individual. If you really believe that you are a *deserving* human being...then giving yourself *permission* to have it all would be the *key to* having it all. It all reverts back to worthiness.

Do you honestly believe you *are* worthy enough to reside in a lean, healthfully configured body? If you don't believe you deserve it, then you'll probably never manifest it for yourself. This is why it's so important to replace our old beliefs and negative self-talk with new positive affirmations. They will be discussed in full detail in the next and final chapter of this book.

THE FORMULA: The science behind the body is just a formula. *Understanding* the formula is something that will help unlock the mystery of how the body actually works. So, I guess that would make *understanding*...the *key*!

After walking yourself through *all of the processes* mentioned in this book...taking care of yourself and making healthy choices will all become second nature.

Part of *my* formula is to throw away your scale. I haven't weighed myself for at least a dozen years or more. I started to think *I was* my number. If a high number would show up on the scale, I would panic, and feel like I had to starve or deprive myself of food. If a low number showed up on the scale, it would give me permission to reward myself with food. How sick is that? The number that showed up on the scale actually ran my life.

My mind had absolutely no *peace* around the subject of food. Finally I understood that food is simply *flavored fuel.* Some flavors are just more appealing to us than others. It's now time to *unlearn our old eating habits* and acquire new desired tastes, to *replace the old ones* we have about food. We need to experiment and do taste tests with a variety of wholesome foods, as if tasting them for the very first time. The best way to do this is to learn how to *savor every morsel* of food you put into your mouth. This means that we must begin chewing each mouthful, as if it's our very last meal *ever.*

Most of us have never really tasted a carrot or a cucumber. You might have gone through the motions by taking a bite, chewing a few times and then gulping down chunks of food. But how often have you really taken a bite, chewed each mouthful, 40 or 50 times, and then gradually allowed it to actually liquefy and begin to be digested by the enzymatic saliva that makes itself available as we chew. Now, go taste a carrot. Begin right now to *enjoy* and chew your food. We all know that some foods make the body feel more energized than others. That stamina will make all the difference in feeling ideal *vs.* run down each and every day. Have you actually experimented with different foods? If not...begin now.

We all know that diets don't work. The only thing that works is to *create a new lifestyle* that supports our positive habits, which will as a whole ultimately turn our life, into one big ongoing pleasant experience!

Breaking old Habits: To break old habits, we must literally change our *thoughts,* as well as the *terminology* or words we choose to use on a daily basis. It took me years of trial and error to finally find the formula that made me feel fabulous. Because I never fully understood what each food did, I had to experiment. There was a time when I *needed* to have a desert after every meal. My body felt ineffective and low on energy by the food choices I made on a daily basis. It felt run down all of the time. Instead of saying "What am I going to eat today?" The new terminology is "What kind of fuel am I going to put in my body today?" What foods will serve me the best? These words will allow you to relate to food differently and in a more suitable way.

Most of us still see food as *comfort* and family related. I remember the best times growing up were always around the kitchen table. That's when my family felt united, congruent, and loving. We need to stop eating food out of *memory,* and begin to see it for what it really is...fuel! You always have the choice to indulge in old habits any time you wish. As long as you remember that you have *a choice,* you can never be upset or blame anyone else.

These days, when I see a gooey casserole dish filled with lots of cheese, butter, and noodles, I'm pretty repulsed, because I actually envision it sticking to my insides, looking like lumpy cottage cheese on my 5-foot frame. I've come to know that "what I see *is* what I get!"

You know that you finally understand *how food* works in your body when you give up the feeling of loss, pain, or deprivation. That's the day, you'll know you hit a home run! Without fully understanding *how* food works in your body, you just can't make conscious willing choices. Once you do fully understand the basics, you'll naturally choose clean, wholesome, nutritious foods, because you love and appreciate them. Be patient with yourself. It's all trial and success! If you stick with it, you *will* get past that point of no return. You'll never again *feel deprived* because your new choice *will* be so nourishing and make you feel so great!

To eat healthfully is simply to eat consciously. To be conscious of something is to be rational, wise, sensible, and discerning. Some people look at *eating healthy* as a "dirty word." You need to give up those *thoughts* or *beliefs* if you want to change your lifestyle, habits and body shape.

Many years ago, I remember going off sugar for a six-week period. I was like an addict kicking the habit…going "cold-turkey," *trying* to diminish the cravings, without instruction, direction, or guidance. After six weeks, I started to incorporate deserts again, and I hated the feeling. It was the first time in over 30 years that I had ever been without sugar. The sugar threw my body and mind into a deranged, unbalanced state. My thoughts were hazy, gloomy, and somber as I went into a state of depression. I didn't know whether I was coming or going. I was completely thrown off balance by the few bites of sugar that I consciously added back into my diet.

Over time, I began to experiment and added a glass of wine, as well as other alcoholic beverages back into my diet. The same thing happened! As soon as I understood that alcohol turns into sugar immediately upon entering the body, it all made perfect sense. I became so sensitive, which at the time seemed like a nightmare but was a blessing in disguise as it "told me" what *wasn't* working. Now, I consciously choose not to drink alcohol or eat many desserts. I just don't like the feeling of grogginess or confusion. The cost is too high. I now love the feeling of clarity, energy and quality. What choices will you make for yourself?

Some people tell me that cutting their portions in half has made all the difference in losing weight. I do believe that smaller portions are very intelligent, however, I see this as a quick fix. It's still a form of deprivation and lack of understanding that *"quality foods* provide fuel, energy and stamina."

If the half portions are filled with dairy, salt, fat, grease, or sugar, then you won't get the effects of feeling energized and nourished. Sure you'll have temporary weight lose, but how are you feeling? Even half portions of these food choices promote diabetes, strokes, heart attacks, and cancer. Once you give up foods for an extended period, and then begin to re-introduce them back into your diet, you'll immediately feel how each individual food effects you. This is why I will speak so forcefully about experimenting with specific foods, later in this chapter.

In the late 70s I was taught the terms *"Yin" and "Yang."* I'll explain only the basics of what these terms imply. Understanding Yin and Yang enabled me to make sense of why my body was thrown into such turbulence. I equate these polar opposites to a pendulum. The far right represents Yin foods and the far left represents Yang foods. One is extremely bitter. The other is extremely sweet. The whole idea is to stick as close to center as possible.

What happens when you eat too much salt is that you'll begin to crave sweets. Likewise, when you eat too much sugar, you'll begin to crave salty or sour foods. Eating close to "center" would be such foods as brown rice, whole grains, beans, fresh vegetables, salads, and fruit. These foods keep your body, mind, and spirit feeling more balanced and centered so that you can produce and perform with consistent high levels of energy throughout each and every day. As soon as you eat something to either extreme, your body is thrown off balance again. It's a vicious cycle. The best we can do is understand, take responsibility, exercise, make conscious choices and experiment with foods until we find our own balance and feel comfort in our own skin.

When I was growing up, my mother had no clue that my blood sugar was low most of the time...scientifically called "hypoglycemia." She also didn't know that I had A.D.D. *(Attention Deficit Disorder).*

All this really *is*, is a deficiency or shortage of attention on any *one* thing at a given time. This precious, unknowing, loving woman would actually feed me cookies, cake, muffins, cereal, or white toast for breakfast. All carbohydrates and no protein! Why didn't she just throw in a pot of coffee, a bottle of booze, and a cigarette to finish me off! So off to school I would go. I'd fall asleep during my first class. The world seemed intolerable and incomprehensible to me. The teacher's lips would move, but I had no clue *what* she was saying. Concentration in my brain was *nonexistent.* I just knew I was the dumbest person in the world. That really devastated my self-esteem!

It was sad, but now I can step out of that situation in my mind's eye and clearly see the alternate paths that could have been taken. But who knew? I felt so lost and alone. Why was this happening? How could anyone let this happen? It's simply ignorance. No one meant anything by it. It's no one's fault. It just seems that no one in "my world" was paying attention as we *transitioned* from harvesting and picking our food *to* bleaching, processing and destroying it. Today, I am quick to understand how this ignorance of *transition to plenty* has contributed to making us one of the dumbest nations in the world around the topic of food.

More people are more obese today than ever before in the history of man. We got caught up in the "sexiness" of *fast food and fast living!* It's not hard to figure out. By "being on the clock" most of our choices have become the *unconscious choice* of "fast." Fast foods are *processed* and laden with fat. Even when you're eating a fast food restaurant's salad, the lettuce is permeated with pesticides and void of nutrients, and then we saturate this near worthless "stuff" with an over-abundance of fatty processed dressing.

We're in such a rushed, fast-paced, gotta' have it now world, that we can no longer see the forest through the trees. We've *lost our perspective* in the transition. Globally, things are changing at the speed of greed, hype, uncaring and ignorance. Unfortunately, other cultures have quickly picked up the error of our ways.

It's overwhelming if we *really* take a look at what's taken place over the past 50 years. The bottom line is that our *healthy choices* are now in the minority, and it takes *time* to eat, especially when you're eating "on the run." Out here in the "real world," as a collective consciousness, we've pretty much set ourselves up to lose. Most of you reading this book are going to have to make *a lot* of conscious choices if you truly want to change your current reality.

So far, I don't see a lot of *agreement* "out there" in the world about setting up more healthy environments for people to live and play in. My entire social life had to change, once I started to consciously choose healthy foods. It's always about choice. The real question shows up as…"What choices have you been making to date that actually make you feel great?" and "What changes do you need to put into action to *have* what you want?" My experience is that we all feel better when we have excellent health. "What are you *willing* to give up to have it all?" I promise you one thing. What *appears* to be "giving up" frequently turns out to have a silver lining. This is a true leap of responsible surrender due only *to faith.*

Would or could we ever go back to our ancestor's *old* ways of thinking? Or, is it now time to just start paying more attention, so that we can intelligently decide for ourselves, which path we really want to take from this point forward? Our thoughts and beliefs need to change *now* if we are ever again to feel invigoratingly in love with life *and* begin to find true comfort in our own skin, if maybe for the first time since birth. These last few years have been so joyous, since I began to take charge of *and* responsibility for, my body. To be able to enjoy each day of life is a wonderful gift. It's available to each and every one of us, just for the asking.

Once you understand this, it all becomes simple. You find out what you already knew. After all, you've heard *the words* at least a hundred times before…"Proper diet, clean air, drink lots of good water, exercise, and take scientifically designed nutritional supplements and *everything* will change in a positive way!" Unfortunately, *understanding it* versus *putting it into action* can be an entirely different ballgame!

I know in my heart, that if my mother had understood that all she needed to do was change my diet and feed me assorted proteins such as eggs, tofu, salmon, or chicken, she gladly would have done that.

She also would have added whole grains, fresh veggies, salad, and fruit. It would have alleviated a lot of grief and pain for everyone. That entire negative childhood experience could have been avoided. Of course then, I couldn't or wouldn't have written this book, and my life would have taken an entirely different course. The cost of our lessons can be huge! I believe we pay with our lives! What's the cost been for you to date? How much more are *you* willing to pay?

I honestly believe that most of us are just missing *a tiny piece of the puzzle*, and that once *that piece* falls into place, our life changes for the better, because it alters the entire picture of our existence. Once you get "the piece," you've got to know the *actions to take,* which is still only *part* of the process...We need to *do the work!* This allows us to enjoy a happy, healthy, conscious existence. Just know the work never ends, because the questions *and* challenges constantly change!

<u>Food Symptoms</u>: Once you *begin* consuming particular foods, you'll quickly notice the *different effects* that each "specific" food has on you. I'm talking about physically *and* mentally. Recognizing and knowing in your mind's eye, *in advance* of putting even a morsel into your mouth, you'll be able to select a specific outcome by the choice you make on a moment by moment basis. I'm not talking about predicting. I'm talking about actually determining how you want to feel and look *in advance* of chewing and swallowing your food. This "understanding" is freedom of choice at it's finest! It's a fabulous experience, and before long, you'll be doing it every day of your life, without having much thought about it. Knowing *what choices to make* will become second nature. Just remember that the circumstances change every day, so we must learn to look at situations in a new way, rather than come from reactive memory, assumption or belief.

Imagine knowing that every day, you actually have the power to create a more gorgeous, healthy, functional body. Who are you going to blame when you *receive* what you want out of life? You can take all the credit, because you've done your homework. The healthy you will just "show up," as you become responsible for "knowing what you know." This kind of autonomy leads to finding comfort in your own skin. I've been on both sides of the coin, and I can honestly tell you that feeling healthy wins every time.

Facts about soda: Doesn't matter if it's diet or regular. It contains phosphorous which throws off the balance of calcium. It actually leeches the calcium out of our bones, teeth, and even our muscles. Why drink something that will destroy the body, when you can stick with water as your drink of choice, which helps cleanse and hydrate the bodily cells.

Regarding alcohol: Bottom line…it immediately turns to sugar as soon as it enters your body. It also destroys your liver, which is a filter. We need a healthy liver, because it aids in the digestive process. Alcohol clouds our thinking and depletes essential vitamin Bs from our cells. Even one glass of wine can distort our thinking for many days after consumption. Why drink something that will destroy the body? It's much easier to stick with water as your drink of choice.

Drink water…plenty of clean, filtered unpolluted water. It helps flush out and release the toxins, excessive salt, sugar, pesticides, poisons, bacteria, viruses, and fat that's stored within the crevices of our body. Never leave home without a bottle of water! Allow your "body of organs" to be quenched throughout each and every day. Your body will love you for it!

Contamination: Every time we eat or drink processed foods, fast foods, fatty/greasy foods, or dairy, we are using our body as a dumping ground and container for destructive fillers and wastes. Since we've been blessed with only one body to last a lifetime, how could we knowingly destroy it? We *can't* "knowingly" destroy it. It all goes back to unawareness *or* missing a piece of the puzzle.

Fast Foods: I am going to use the general term "fast food" as a guideline of what you're better off living without: They consist of…

- Deep fried foods
- Anything high in *saturated* fats (there *are* good fats!) I use *OptOmega Oil.*
- Refined carbohydrates (which turn into sugar)
- Processed foods (especially white processed - void of nutrition)

- Foods with "low fat" labels (usually have a very high sugar content)
- Dairy (cheese, butter, ice cream)
- Soda (includes diet soda) and all other drinks laden with sugar.

There's old rancid fat lurking in almost every area of your body, and it's just screaming to escape. This contaminated fat shows up in many ways, such as diabetes, cancer, strokes, heart attacks, lethargy, arthritis, glaucoma, migraines, and depression, just to name a few. Making conscious choices pretty much could have prevented any of these diseases.

<u>What can we do differently</u>? We can graze! The truth is…I eat all day long, and I currently live in the reality of a size 6. We all have "stuff" to work through, so the key is to make your body feel full *and* satisfied all day long so you can avoid the pitfall of becoming ravenous around food. Never leave home without having water and healthy snacks in a temperature resistant container.

Listen to your body and *eat* when it says, *"I'm hungry."* Graze all day long, *continuously* nibbling on very small quantities of satisfying foods that make you feel good. It's a good thing! Give your body fuel that allows you to sail smoothly throughout the day.

Take it one day at a time. Of course you'll occasionally test yourself by eating foods that don't serve you, because you've *rigged up* some *fond memory* from your past to coincide with this type of eating. You're only human and perfection can get boring, so give yourself a break with forgiveness and begin again. When you fall off a horse, you've gotta' get right back on or *fear* sets in. Just get in touch with your truth and re-choose it.

Even before going to a party be sure you're hunger is *already* satisfied *before* you arrive. Even a glass of water will help curb your appetite. If you don't set yourself up to win, you'll most likely become a human vacuum cleaner by eating platefuls of greasy, salty, overly processed food. Being already satisfied will allow you to nibble on your favorite foods from whatever selection is offered.

Let's face the facts! We *feel* better when we don't cram in large amounts of food at one sitting. It puts undue stress on the entire body. To breathe into a heavy, rich meal is painful because the digestive process is just plain exhausting. How good do you *really* feel after eating large portions? Personally, I don't like to feel sluggish, heavy, or irritable!

I love how easily fresh fruits, salads, and vegetables are digested. Also, they make you feel light, balanced, and centered. Life feels more worth living when you feel that good.

Go ahead...graze all day long. Eat very small portions whenever you like. Just pay attention and *choose* what you put in. You won't feel guilty if your original choice was a *conscious* choice.

Never starve yourself or skip meals. Occasionally it's okay to go on a *supervised* fast, (which is not starving yourself). The foods and liquids you choose to consume will make a tremendous difference in your attitude and ultimate well-being. Set yourself up to win.

Aside from the foods mentioned above, every morning I blend non-fat soymilk with USANA'S *Almond Fibergy Powder, Soyamax Protein Powder* and *OptOmega 3* and *6 Oil,* which provides "essential fatty acids." Occasionally I'll add ice and fruit. The meal/snack bars, also provided by Usana, are not to be missed. They're satisfying, nutritious, delicious, and *are all* certified low-glycemic which means they are balanced and will not throw you into a sugar high/sugar blues situation. Set yourself up to win every day of your life.

Imagine never again having the need to feel uncomfortable around food because you've taken charge of your "diet." This will allow confidence instead of doubt. Over time your body will be *clear* about the messages it is receiving. The leaner you become, the easier it is to decipher the messages.

The truth is, sometimes you're just going to feel more ravenous than others. The most significant thing to know is... *what* you're eating. The other crucial piece of information is the *sequence* in which you are consuming food. Don't ever again *fear* food. The *functions* of a variety of foods will become obvious to you over time.

Some people choose to consciously combine their foods. The first time I ever heard of "conscious combining" was over 20 years ago. I read about it in "The Beverly Hills Diet" book. I don't ever recommend diets by the way. What I do recommend is acquiring knowledge and changing your lifestyle, by changing your thoughts, food choices, and exercise habits. I take my constantly accumulated knowledge and incorporate it into my current lifestyle by picking and choosing what does and does not work. Combing science, common sense, and experience is fun *and* satisfying.

To understand "conscious combining," we must first understand how different *types* of foods digest differently in the human body. Dairy products consist of protein and fat. Dairy takes longer to digest than any other food group. It takes anywhere from 12 to 24 hours for your body to process and digest cheese, cream, butter, and other rich sources of dairy. Quite simply, it creates mucus. Even once the dairy products are digested, you still have to deal with the process of *burning fat* that the dairy puts into your body. If it's not burned off (via deep breathing or exercise), it will store up and make you look large and lumpy like cottage cheese. No matter how you look at it, it's not a pretty sight, unless you live in Alaska, and use the fat as a protective coat or shield against extreme weather conditions. I *chose* to give up dairy. You can choose to do whatever you want. Remember...there are no "have to's," as long as you understand the *consequences* of your choices.

The Dairy Industry told us to drink and eat mucus, pus, bacteria and hormones from a cow and called it milk, cheese, butter, and ice cream. What could they have been thinking? I'm sure we've just accepted traditional customs and habits from our ancestors. We've been programmed for so long, that we actually eat and drink things without questioning. Volumes have been written to cover the topic of dairy foods. If you want more information on how dairy affects the human body, just go to www.notmilk.com. Warning: I'm sure you'll be repulsed if you look at this website, but I experimented with dairy in my own body way before I ever heard about this website and my experience is that it clogs our system and undermines our health and well-being.

The opposite end of the digestive process is <u>fruit</u>. Fruit mostly consists of water, fiber and fructose or fruit sugar. Most fruits only take 1 to 2 hours to digest. You eat it, and before you know it, it's gone. Many fruits also contain natural enzymes that aid in digestion, as well as antioxidants. They can also assist in burning excess fat if combined in the proper sequence with other foods. This is where the "conscious combining" process really rocks!

Let's say you ate a heavy, fatty, greasy meal 4 to 6 hours earlier. At this point, it's *perfect* to eat an enzyme-laden fruit, such as strawberries, mangos, kiwis or pineapple. If you were to eat the fruit immediately following the heavy meal, it could not get past the previously consumed dish, because of the *amount of time* it takes to digest fats and proteins. The fruit then becomes stuck in a traffic jam behind the heavy dairy or protein, and it begins to ferment. This fermentation process will create pockets of gas, which would not only feel uncomfortable inside of your body, but might also prove to be embarrassing in a social situation. One more thing to point out is that the fruit that is fermenting behind the protein is beginning to turn to sugar, which then turns to fat, so you end up gaining weight from the fruit. This entirely counteracts its purpose in nature. To knowingly put your body in this situation is a disservice.

<u>Vegetables</u> are next in line of the most easily digested foods. The body eliminates vegetables in approximately 3 hours. Vegetables are also high in fiber, so they aid in the elimination process, which ultimately assists in cleansing the colon. The colon needs to remain clean and healthy. Diseases can be initiated in the colon unless the toxins are flushed out and eliminated that have built up over time.

<u>Proteins</u>, other than dairy, consist of meat, chicken, fish, nuts, grains, and soy. Soy is the most easily digested protein that may take approximately 3 to 4 hours to digest. Seafood digests in 4 to 5 hours depending on its consistency. Chicken may take 5 hours and meat up to 7 hours.

<u>Grains</u> consist of protein and carbohydrates, so the average digestion time could be anywhere from 4 to 6 hours.

Anytime you make changes in your lifestyle, you can usually count on *withdrawal symptoms.* This is why choice is so very important. If you're changing for *someone else* and *not* yourself, then *blame* and *failure* due to lack of results will most likely occur. Take the necessary time when making any changes. And, don't make the change until you are ready!

When you want to make healthy choices, adding foods that quickly burn as fuel, make the most sense. My choices are usually foods that digest quickly, as well as organic foods grown locally. Cookies, spaghetti or rice cakes just don't get it! They're just fillers and they provide no nutritional value. Think things *all the way through* before making purchases. Don't fall into the trap of "purchasing foods for the household, that set you up to lose!" Always have available fresh assorted fruits, a fresh variety of leafy vegetables, whole grains, pure lean proteins, such as soy/tofu, cold water fish, skinless chicken breasts, raw unsalted nuts and complex carbohydrates prepared and ready to eat at all times! Eating uncooked, raw foods is best. Allow your self "time" to cultivate a taste for this kind of clean eating, especially if you're used to eating deep-fried or processed foods.

The more fiber and roughage you eat, the more naturally your colon will become cleansed. This flushing is vital, because if blocked, the colon can become a haven for toxins that ultimately give birth to disease.

<u>Learning *how* to shop</u>: Before I was aware of how important nutrition really is, I got caught up in the glamorous adventure of eating in restaurants on a daily basis. I was so lazy that I stopped shopping for food and fell into the rut of no longer cooking and preparing my own food. I completely lost touch with reality regarding wholesome, nutritious foods. It's amazing how subtle those inches and pounds start adding up and piling on. I was oblivious to the layers of fat that gradually adhered to my body *without discrimination.* I gained 2 clothe sizes before I woke up and realized that until I took control of *what* I put into my body, I was leaving myself to *chance* as well as unintelligent habits. After all, who *are* these people who are actually preparing meals in restaurants?

159

No matter how conscious the restaurant chefs are, do they really care how much butter, fat, salt, or sugar they throw into a frying pan, while preparing *anyone's* meal? Would they have a clue or even care what you already consumed on that day or any other day? Don't get me wrong...lots of restaurants are *great*, but we need to do *everything* in life within reason. We need to pay attention to possible consequences that will occur as a result of our actions. Usually this only takes a little knowledge mixed with a bit of common sense.

Knowing that I needed to change my lifestyle, I finally decided to take charge of my body. This meant visiting a place that had become foreign to me. After a dozen plus years of having *others* prepare my food, I went to a *grocery store*. Can you imagine that cavemen never experienced the conveniences of anything even remotely similar to a grocery store? How easy it is to take things for granted in this fast-paced world that we now live in.

At first, I was like a kid in a candy shop. What I saw was really fabulous. Of course there was an array of fresh *everything* from all parts of the world. The difference I experienced in this grocery store is that I saw it in a *new* way that I had never experienced before. I learned to shop the outer rim of the store, because that's where all of the fresh foods are located. It sounds so insignificant, but this was *new* for me. It broke my old habit of rushing to the canned, frozen, and shelved processed foods.

The *basics* of conscious eating are overall, a no-brainer. Of course, we all know we're supposed to eat fresh fruit, vegetables and proteins low in saturated fat, but do we really understand why? The *clogging* process that takes place is amazing. It's no wonder we're living in an age where a huge percentage of our society is obese and riddled with diseases such as diabetes, strokes, cancer, arthritis, migraines, glaucoma, and heart attacks. If you analyze all of these diseases, it's common sense to see that the same factors contribute to every one of them. Call it what you will, but no matter how you look at it, obstruction, impediments, blockage, constriction, congestion, and clogging are all caused by foods and toxins we've chosen to eat, which in turn create barriers to having our bodies function the way nature designed them to. We need to grow up and take responsibility for what we choose to put in.

If you feed an all-vegetable diet to a carnivore, they're most likely going to die sooner than later. If you eat enough bottom feeders, (shrimp, crab, and lobster), you're gonna' get sick sooner than later. If you put sugar in the gas tank of your car, it's gonna' conk out sooner than later. It doesn't show up much differently in the body. Why not use fructose (fruit sugar) instead of white processed sugar? If you smoke cigarettes I can tell you right now that the human body was not designed to digest tar. It's just gonna' stick to your lungs until the oxygen can't get through. Lets face it...if you continue to abuse your body...those impurities will build up. If you're not lucky enough to die, you'll most likely suffer a long drawn out, very expensive, slow motion, uncomfortable death, from one of the man-made diseases, listed above.

It's *not* fun to be *or* feel sick. It restricts you from living the life you want. Begin shopping deliberately and intelligently. Search for wholesome foods with very little fat, sugar, salt, or processing. Buy *fresh* foods rather than canned. I began looking at the color white as the enemy. I'm talking about white, processed, non-nourishing fillers. Think about it...white flour, white sugar, ice cream, butter, lard, and fat. These foods bring *a new meaning* to the word "clogging!"

The bottom line is that we must allow food to be our fuel and nourishment as it was originally designed to be. Only buy snacks that keep you and the entire family satisfied and healthy. Ultimately that's one of the major things that will set you up to win. If you buy a pound of candy you already know whose going to eat it. Choose *fuel foods* that will energize and sustain you and your family, rather than thick rich foods that overburden and under nourish you to the point of exhaustion and disease.

No one needs to go "cold turkey"; that would *really* be deprivation and setting yourself up to fail. We simply need to remember that it took us years to learn all our old habits and we don't need to give up everything at once. **Gradually** *replace* old habits with new ones to

161

minimize symptoms of withdrawal. REMEMBER…it's always a matter of choice!

I often compare the human body to a trash compactor. We fill it with a random assortment of so-called foods, and then expect our body to process this huge amount of food and disappear it into thin air. After swallowing the food, it has only one place to go…and that's the stomach. Even though we can actually *see* the stomach protruding on most people, it was originally designed to be the size of a fist. My point is…we've stretched the stomach so much, that we have now become a society where we have "agreement" to be immense and diseased, as if it's expected and "normal." It all seems we've accepted overeating and illness as a way of life.

Heavy meals are just too difficult to digest. They clog the system and create discomfort inside our "mini-me." We are destroying our child within. My final word on this topic is that eating any heavy foods late at night can disturb sleep patterns by creating extremely annoying, disruptive dreams throughout the night. The digestive process makes the body work too hard!

How you start your day makes all the difference in the world. Be sure you begin with the proper amount of protein, the right kind of carbohydrates, no processed white sugars or honey, and the right kind of fats. The right foods and vitamins minimize and eliminate cravings.

<u>Nourishment, a*re you worth the price of conscious foods? YES…*</u> *you bet you are!* ☺   Forget what you ever learned about eating. It's time to start over with scientific information that produces desired results. Most parents only had basic information, and the majority of that was inaccurate. Today we're living in an information age, which makes intelligent choices much easier.

Being coherent and able to concentrate has become a priority in my life. I invite you to *begin experimenting* with foods, as I did, so that you will be able to specifically know what foods make you feel clear, fresh and happy, versus foods that take you under. Since we know that proteins and fats take longer to digest than other foods, we can be assured that we will have a feeling of being full and satisfied for much longer. Eliminating saturated fats is a wise idea. I personally use extra virgin olive oil, roasted sesame oil, and *OptOmega Oil* which contains flax, omega 3 and omega 6 EFA (never cook with this oil).

Experiment: Actually find out for yourself if what the dairy industry says is true about dairy products. For one week, go out and eat cheese, milk, butter, ice cream, white bread, white rice, white sugar, cereal and spaghetti. Pay attention for the next few days and see how you feel. Hopefully you'll live through the experiment, as these are foods that help promote heart disease, strokes, cancer, diabetes, arthritis, glaucoma, etc.

Does your saliva have a thick consistency? How's your energy level? Is your nasal passage blocked? How's your breathing? Do you feel like you could run a marathon? Keep listening to your body. It never lies! Our body was not designed to digest the bodily fluids of a cow or any animal for that matter.

Drinking water is wonderful, but even it can't wash mucus out of your body. This is where conscious combining plays a major role. Because if you do choose to continue eating fast foods rich in dairy, the enzymes contained in pineapple, strawberries, papaya, or kiwi's can at least assist in burning and cutting through the possible damage that's already been done. Remember that fruit ferments and it can't get through, so wait a while before adding fruit to your over stuffed and compacted digestive system, as it will already be blocked by the heavy fat and sugar-laden foods mentioned above.

Keep experimenting: If you managed to live through the fat phase of the experiment, it's time to go to the next level. For the next week, introduce the foods that make you feel wonderful. Eat fresh salads for a week with a variety of organic greens and your favorite fresh vegetables (without all of those fancy, thick, processed dressings). Remember to chew each morsel so that it dissolves and digests in your mouth. This will allow you to detect the delicious flavor of *each* vegetable.

Mix your own dressing. I use unsaturated oil, Balsamic vinegar, lemon pepper, and any other herbs and spices that tickle my fancy.

163

Don't forget the proteins that are essential in building muscles, such as nuts, baked tofu, baked salmon, or skinless chicken breast. Pay attention...how do you feel now? How's your energy level and stamina? You may very well begin to experience withdrawal symptoms. Remember Yin and Yang...eating at extremely opposite ends of the food chain will throw your body out of sync. That causes cravings, so be prepared by replacing the old food habits with new ones immediately. I began drinking Usana meal replacement drinks and eating their delicious lean nutrition bars to balance and alleviate my cravings back in 1994. This has set me up to win, by always having the right foods available *before* I'm suffering hunger pangs. Remember...*never* shop when you're hungry.

It's important to know that turkey contains tryptophan, an essential amino acid. Tryptophan affects people in different ways. For me, it's like a drug. It puts me to sleep within minutes of touching my pallet. Having hypoglycemia has allowed me to become very sensitive to and aware of the effects of imbalances in my blood sugar. The symptoms are...grogginess and passing out. This isn't brain surgery. Learning these easily obvious pieces of information about how foods affect you personally can turn your life around. It allows you to make conscious choices, so that if there are any side affects, you already know what's coming. And, you can't blame anyone else. You get to take full responsibility, which is truly a gift. This *knowing* and *understanding* will keep you from being on automatic pilot or functioning like a robot.

<u>Visualization</u>: Once you truly understand how foods make you feel, and exactly which "symptoms" *occur* by consuming each mouthful of food...you can begin to use the process of "visualization" to your benefit. Every time I see fried or fatty fast foods, I immediately envision exactly how each food will make me look and feel, *in advance* of buying it. I actually see a photograph in my mind's eye of how I will look if I eat that particular food, versus making a more intelligent choice.

For example, if I walk into a market and smell the aroma of freshly fried chicken, I immediately go to the counter and *look* at the fried chicken. I imagine eating that greasy, unhealthy food that used to be associated with a fond memory. I then *envision* my fat cells swelling up throughout my entire body, wherein every cell of my body is drenched with fat, because it absorbed every ounce of lard contained in that piece of chicken. Also, I envision myself feeling uncomfortable and lethargic, because I have just outgrown the pants that used to fit comfortably. At the end of this quick visualization process, if I still wish to eat the piece of chicken, I will. And, I won't even feel guilty or want to blame anyone, because it was truly my conscious choice. Even *unwise* choices should be *conscious* choices. It's hard to ever go back, once you understand something clearly.

Now, let's continue the visualization process. Every time you see a luscious, green, organic salad with assorted raw leafy green fresh vegetables, and lean protein...see your mind and body becoming excited about the possibilities of feeling and looking extraordinary. See your body releasing and dissolving excess fat and replacing it with lean, muscle mass, as you enjoy each memorable healthy bite of this meal designed for a king. You now feel more energy and stamina than you've ever conceived possible. Knowing that you have found and chosen to use the key to unlock true, vibrant health.

Lovingly shop for, wash and prepare your foods. Show appreciation and respect for every delectable morsel you consume. Never again take for granted how easy it is to have access to grocery stores where we can purchase fresh organic foods of our choice, rather than having to hunt and farm, as our ancestors did. Understand how pure, organic food is brimming with essential nutrients. Smelling and digesting a freshly chopped salad is truly an experience of eating from God's Garden. It's an adventure not to be missed.

Once you begin savoring your food in this way you will never be able to return to abruptly inhaling your meals. You will never again allow yourself to be caught up in the busy-ness of the daily routine or rut. Rushing into fast food restaurants is no longer an option. We just don't go there. We now take the necessary time to shop and prepare our meals in advance. This will set you and your family up to win

I thought it would be best to paint an old paradigm (or pattern) of the way I used to live my life...vs. the life *I choose* to live today, since a lot of us are visual and see things in pictures.

165

<u>A typical day in my life *before* conscious choices</u>:

An alarm would blast away at 7:00 a.m. I'd jump out of bed and quickly down a pot of coffee, accompanied by cake or cookies as I rushed around the house preparing myself to drive in rush-hour traffic to a job I despised. On the weekend, if I was lucky...I'd go out for a big man-sized breakfast with my friends. It would consist of fried eggs and potatoes with bacon and white toast with gobs of butter. I was so frazzled by the time I arrived at work...I needed "soothing." Anyone who has ever been overweight will know that I was about to eat something to make myself feel better. It could have been a hamburger or a milkshake. I know for sure that whatever it was...it *wasn't* in my best interest!

All day long, I'd eat on the run, gobbling, nibbling and chewing away, trying to pass the time until I could leave the job that I hated. Again, I'd be in rush hour traffic, of course stopping along the way to drive through a fast-food restaurant. It was very easy for me to consume a few big burgers, fries, and a milkshake.

Once in a while, I would replace the shake for hot apple pie, cookies, or chocolate candy. I was so clueless! By the time I arrived home, I was thoroughly exhausted. So, of course, rather than choose to exercise, I'd take a nap. When I woke up from the nap, I'd usually be hungry again, so the vicious cycle would continue. I was feeling weaker and sicker as day turned to night.. I knew I was in trouble by the time I hit 30 years of age. Life was just no longer worth living in the state I was in. Finally, after many years, I became so tired of being sick and tired, that I was ready to make any and all changes that were necessary to feel true health.

<u>Here' a typical day in my new designer lifestyle</u>:

I wake up naturally and peacefully to the sound of birds chirping. I gently roll out of bed and slip on my walking or work-out shoes. I make my morning drink, which consists of the following ingredients mixed in a blender...warmed low-fat soy milk; a half-cup of decaffeinated coffee; USANA *Almond Fibergy* powder; their *Soyamax* protein powder; and a few big squirts of their refrigerated *oil* which contains essential fatty acids which are crucial to cardiovascular health.

I then walk to my office, which is a very large sunroom overlooking my tropical garden in the back of my home. Life becomes really beautiful as I sit down to compose my book, or conduct miscellaneous business.

Watching the tiny animals frolicking in the yard inspires me. After writing for a few hours, my stomach growls for food. I've set myself up to win, so I walk to the kitchen where I'm able to make easy choices. Fresh salmon, free-range organically fed chicken breasts and hard-boiled eggs that I prepared earlier in the week await me. There's also brown rice already prepared in the steamer and fresh greens and raw vegetables in the frig...just waiting to be consumed by me later in the day, or whenever I'm in the mood to eat.

My salads are assorted with organic veggies such as arugula, baby spinach, baby romaine, tomatoes, cucumbers, sprouts, beans, broccoli, and whatever else is available. I sprinkle lemon pepper, balsamic vinegar and oil sparingly onto the salad and indulge. It is amazingly delicious. I chew each morsel until it has dissolved, and then, I go back to my computer and write some more. A few hours later I may feel I'm ready for a break. So, I walk into the bedroom where I have created a peaceful, private space for myself. I put on music and consciously breathe deeply for as long as it seems necessary. While I'm breathing, I pick up my weights and either do isometrics, aerobics, or whatever my body wants. After all, I'm already wearing the perfect shoes, which set me up to win each and every day. Whether I choose to exercise or not is entirely up to me. I've come to learn however, that choosing to exercise will make me feel much more energized and invigorated.

When I'm done exercising, I put on a meditation CD, by Michele Blood. I prefer her affirmations and meditations to others I've heard, because she inspires me to be the best I can be. I'm reminded of my magnificence when I listen to her words. She reminds me of *who* I am, and *where* I'm going. I also love listening to her *Laughing Meditation CD*. This brings me into such a playful, grateful state.

Hearing the contagious laughter reminds me of how innocence is always at our fingertips and that we're only just a laugh or smile away from feeling peace, love, and joy. It also reminds me not to ever take anything or anyone *too* seriously.

When I'm finished exercising and meditating, I like to soak in the hot tub with my delicious aromatic oils and scented candles burning throughout the rooms. I also give myself a facial at least once a week. After this quality time I like to watch the *Dr. Phil* and *Oprah* shows whenever possible. By this time, I've taken care of myself. I've allowed myself to be creative. I've put in a full day, and I'm ready to visit with my mate whose office is at the other end of our home. We usually go out for a light healthy meal.

My favorite restaurants are where Mediterranean *and* oriental foods are served. A few times a week, we treat ourselves to a *Starbucks'* decaf, soy, latte'. That's pretty harmless compared to a lot of their specialty drinks that are dosed with sugary syrups, milk, and cream. During the day and or as a nighttime snack, I nibble on fresh fruit or *USANA'S* certified low-glycemic nutrition bars, drinks and supplements. They provide lasting energy, they taste delicious and are easy to digest.

It all boils down to what you're willing to "give up" as well as "incorporate into your life." Are you willing to have it all? Are you willing to break away from the beliefs that were instilled in you for so very long? What changes are you *willing* to make? Are you willing to take the road less traveled? The choice is always yours. If you choose a certain path because you felt pressured by someone else, then...you didn't choose! If you're blaming others for the hand you were dealt, then you certainly didn't choose. You'll have what you want, as soon as you take full responsibility. Remember...you are *not* a victim, unless you choose to be! Do the necessary work to have what you want!

Nothing comes from nothing! You are so worth having the best of everything in life...especially the healthy, lean, energetic body of your dreams. If you have children, you must still make and take special time for yourself, even if it's only a few minutes each day.

This will not only preserve your sanity, but also help maintain the joy and balance of your family.

I've personally had to learn not to schedule too many things on my calendar. It tends to interrupt the quality of my day. It also breaks the flow of my creativity. Sometimes I won't answer the phone for an entire week. Of course I'll check messages in case a matter needs immediate attention. I'll return calls, as deemed appropriate.

You can see why I purposefully left this chapter until almost last...because if you don't address your *issues* first, then you are simply placing a *Band-Aid* over a wound that cries out for attention, which might otherwise never heal properly. We are not fragmented or divided up into parts. We are whole and complete as body, mind, and spirit and must deal with the whole *before* going outside of ourselves. How can we deeply touch others without first finding comfort in our own skin?

In today's modern world of technology, every form of information is now easily and quickly available to us on every topic imaginable. To find out *who* you truly are and *what* you really love, begin now to make the essential time for yourself and do the work while there *is* still time. I never believed that life provided the time to do all of the things that we love. The truth is, the more I take care of myself...the more fun life becomes. There's no shortage of time. We all have the same 24-hour period, 7 days each week, all year 'round. What are you doing with yours? Take responsibility for the choices you make.

Begin living each moment, rather than putting it off for a "tomorrow" that never comes. Put a whole new twist on *your* today. Give yourself permission to re-claim your life and have fun now.

I've had to learn that we don't always get everything *exactly* when we want it! But, that we will get *what we want* through the lessons of faith, belief, positive thoughts, and never giving up! Speak the affirmations in the next and final chapter of this book as often as possible. Make the time...for this will allow you to speak your new designer life into existence.

What are you telling yourself?

"When you have a disease, do not identify with it
Or try to fix it. Find your center of wholeness
And you will be healed."

- Chinese Proverb

Affirmations and Visualizations!
...Changing your Thoughts *and* your Words _will_ Change your Life.

> No matter what I say
> ...Life always says, "you are right!"
> Let me show you some evidence of that.
> From now on,
> I choose to talk only about how good life is
> And how fortunate I am.
> I always get more of whatever I appreciate!
> From now on,
> I choose to appreciate *everything* I want more of!
>
> - Jacquelyn Aldana

I believe that to reinvent the wheel is a total waste of time, so I asked my good friend and twin-soul sister Michele Blood for permission to draw from a lot of her work in this chapter. Because of her commitment to serve and forward mankind, she was only too happy to say yes, and I deeply appreciate her for allowing me to do this. The following quote from Brian Tracy sums up how masterfully Michele helps people worldwide change their lives for the better.

> *"Michele has put together materials that bring about permanent behavioral change. There is something in the human being that is naturally drawn by music, and you don't need to have any musical ability. All you have to do is hear the message combined with the music, and it becomes part of you forever."*
>
> - Brian Tracy

Powerful affirmations will allow your heart to sing, for your words *do* determine your outcome in life! Are you thinking happy, healthy, wealthy thoughts? Positive words and thoughts will help motivate you to the highest levels of achievement. An affirmation is something you repeat over and over and over again. Regardless of whether it's negative or positive, it will reinforce your subconscious mind to think, act, and ultimately *be* a specific way. What you tell yourself on a minute by minute basis is so important. Choosing positive thoughts is just as easy as choosing any other kind of thought, so why not write a positive script for yourself?

Expand your imagination and begin telling yourself specific affirmations that do not place limitations on the way you want your life to unfold. You can become just about anything and everything you wish to be. Just say the accurate words! The *terms* we use are so essential. Have fun with your life, your words *and* your actions. Don't take yourself too seriously. Believe me...no one else does! Give yourself permission to reach for the moon.

Visualize yourself *already* being, doing, and having anything and everything you've wished for. Walt Disney used his imagination. He always saw everything in his mind's eye before he actually attained it. He and his creative team started each day by affirming that they were using their creative imaginations to achieve the best cartoons, theme parks, TV shows, and movies. They were *affirming, visualizing* and *goal-setting* all at the same time. This is a very powerful combination, for we begin to vibrate at a higher frequency. The more we do this, the closer we come to attaining and achieving our goals.

Repeating our desires *frequently* is paramount. So constantly expand your vision by adding fun things. Never give up on your dreams, for life is so worth living when you're doing what you love.

I've had to apply a certain degree of discipline in my life in order to achieve certain goals, but maintaining spontaneity and having lots of fun is always at the forefront. Live a lot and live out loud! Remember what Terry Cole Whittaker said... *"What other people think of me is none of my business!"*

If you are having challenges with visualizing, you can purchase an effective and inspirational poster at **www.MusiVation.com**. It's called *"My Magnetic Future-Self Board."* You can also invest in a large piece of cardboard and draw a big magnet on it. Inside the magnet, write down your affirmations, for example...

- I (_____), give thanks to my higher power, knowing that I am a magnet to all that is good. I see it, I feel it, I am it, and so it is!" (Now sign your name.)

Inside the magnet, start gluing all of the things you want to attract to yourself...houses, cars, pictures of money, and anything else you desire. Right in the middle, paste a picture of yourself. If you want to release excess weight, say something like...

- "I am now at my perfect weight." (Affirm it as if it's *already* occurred!)

Cut out a picture of a body you think is beautiful and paste your face on it. This is very powerful! It's *your* dream board, so make it up the way you want *your* reality to be. Look at this picture everyday and know it's already a done deal. Before long, you'll automatically begin to take the necessary actions for maintaining your perfect body, such as exercising and eating healthier.

Eventually you'll get what you've visualized and asked for. In fact, we're always *already* visualizing and what's presently in our lives *is* a result of what we've visualized in the past. Now...it's simply a matter of consciously and intentionally visualizing what we want. **Never** visualize what you don't want, only visualize what you do want and, always in the present tense as if it's already happened. For example, don't say...*"I need to lose weight!"* Instead say..."I am at my perfect weight." Your results and experience will conform to your vocabulary. Before you know it, fruits and vegetables *are* more attractive and appealing to you than fatty, greasy, unhealthy alternatives.

A luxury car is another example. Visit various car dealerships wearing your finest attire. Don't forget to take your camera along. Have your photo taken standing beside *and* sitting behind the wheel of your dream car. Be sure to paste this photo in the center of your magnet board.

Also...on a blank check, write in the amount of money that you want to attract. Be sure to put your name as the recipient, and be sure to *sign* the check..."God, the Universal Banker" and *date* the check "perfect time." The universe will comply! Continually visualize yourself having the money, the houses, the cars and the perfect healthy body, knowing that God or whomever the universal

173

power is to you... *is* your supplier. Also, change the board, as your vision becomes bigger. Make it happen now and enjoy your life.

I've talked a lot about the *mind* throughout this book. The mind represents all those tiny voices that speak to us constantly. It's a nagging reminder of all of the undermining undertones we've incorporated and accumulated into our subconscious over time which is why *positive affirmations* are so important.

Take control of your life now and begin *affirming* over and over again all that you *already* own in your heart. Confirm your beliefs *before* they physically appear. It is your decision to choose what to tell yourself. Remember... your subconscious mind is subjective and will believe *everything* you tell it. So speak to yourself *positively* from this day forward!

Even when I was very much in debt, I allowed myself to feel wonderful and rich! We can't allow our *circumstances* to dictate or determine our future. What really matters is *what we are telling ourselves*, which is *why* affirmations are so important.

There is no need ever to compete or compare yourself with anyone. You are a unique individual, so be authentic and true to yourself. The truth is, people don't know *who* you are until you *show* them. You can re-create and re-invent yourself at any given moment. *Everything* conforms to the words you choose to use. Remember that ultimately, life is all about "*agreement!*" The minute you say something, things will begin to correspond to your words, and changes begin to occur... and not a minute sooner! Just because you *used to be* a certain way, does not mean that you need to stay that way or continue on down that old boring path.

Growth comes when you *get in touch* with all that you presently have, so write down what you're already grateful for and then you can add to and build onto that... *any* future you choose for yourself. This will keep everything in perspective and build a strong foundation or platform to start from!

The good news is that you actually get to *make it all up* as you go, because when you *change your thinking*... you change your energy patterns, which ultimately changes your life!

Affirmations are the final missing link and key to *your* happiness. They will allow you to clean up the negative *mind chatter* that has been handed down from generation to generation. Check in to see what you're telling yourself on a daily basis. What words do you use?

Here are a few of the affirmations I use regularly. Be sure to say affirmations in the "present" tense *as if* they're already happening.

- Miracles are happening to me *right now* and everyday!

- I love, accept, and forgive myself!

- I am a loving and forgiving person!

- I am successful and I love who I am!

- I am the master of my destiny!

- I live a balanced, centered, serene, happy, healthy life on a daily basis!

- Faith and belief stimulate and fuel my dreams!

- My dreams are always fully realized!

- I give thanks that my wonderful perfect mate is now in my life!

- I always love and accept others to be who they are!

- My response is always loving!

- I *now* have more money than I'll ever need or require!

- I always give thanks for the joys and gifts of life!

- I am always grateful for living my life in true freedom, honesty and integrity!

- I attract prosperity!

- I am grateful for always having clarity, choice, wisdom and true mental balance!

- I am always generous with myself and others!

- I am prosperous, wealthy and open to receive in all areas of my life!

- My honesty brings me great fortune, and I accept my rightful abundance!

- I always deserve money and have unlimited potential!

- I am now debt-free and always have more money than I need or could ever spend!

- I am always grateful for having time to live!

- My income always exceeds my needs!

- I am always divinely guided to be in the right place at the right time!

- I always attract perfect people who love contributing to my life and well-being...as I do for them!

- I am blessed to always receive everything that I ask for with gratitude.

- The perfect people, places and things are always placed on my path to contribute to my life in positive ways!

- My prayers and needs are always answered and met at the perfect time!

- Everything I do is easy, effortless, and with ease and grace!

- Everything I do is filled with love, joy and peace!

- I choose to live in the now, trusting life will show me how!

- The perfect people are always magnetized and attracted to me!

- I trust in life to guide and carry me away to my highest good!

- I appreciate my body...but I am more than my body...I am a Powerful Spirit!

- I love and accept myself and eat only the foods that are good for me!

- I am energy. I exercise regularly!

- My body is healthy and full of life!

- My healthy body is the vehicle with which I experience the world!

- I am a magnet to money in all forms!

- Money is my obedient servant!

- I freely distribute and circulate what I have...there are no shortages!

- I know that I am prosperous and that all good comes back to me abundantly!

- I now have time to achieve all of my true goals and I am debt free!

- I am a magnet to money, I now have more than I need!

- I always give thanks for my spacious, beautiful, calm and serene home!

- Where I live, always exceeds my dreams and is spacious, beautiful, calm and serene!

- I now own all of my homes...debt-free!

- I always have *at least* 10 multiple streams of income!

- Perfect housing always exceeds my needs!

- My words have power!

- My life always has joy, purpose, and meaning!

- Action converts my goals into reality!

- Only good comes into my life now!

- I always think positive thoughts!

- I release what I no longer want!

- I always know what choices to make in every situation!

- I fully experience every moment in a positive way!

- I always live my life in a happy and satisfying manner!

- I create my life and I'm responsible for changing my thoughts!

- I remain true to myself!

- I love myself!

- I am prosperous in all that is good!

- I am always filled with love, harmony, peace and joy!

- I have a consciousness of abundance and easily receive all good that comes to me!

- My hunches and intuitions are always accurate!

- My dreams always become a reality!

- My grand visions create my reality!

- I am focused and centered at all times!

- My attitude is always positive!

- I always maintain a high level of energy!

- It is easy for me to flow with the rhythm of life!

- I now have the ability and skills to create all that I need or want!

- My goals are always clearly defined!

- I always do what I love which serves others and me!

- I surrender to my higher power, knowing that I am *always* being well taken care of!

Make great use of every minute…even if you're just driving to and from work! That's a wonderful time to pop a *book on tape* or one of Michele Blood's audiocassettes or CDs into the player and sing along. I love her work! Below are just a few of her songs from *"Be a Magnet to Money."*

– THIS DAY –

"I greet this day with love in my heart.
I am living this day as if it was my last.
Today I begin a new life!
Today my life has a new start!
I greet this day with love in my heart!"
*(The melody that Michele puts to this song is so sweet)!

– BORN RICH –

I was born to live this way…I was born rich!
I was born to live this way…I set my goals today!
I was born to live this way…and rich I'm going to stay!
'Cause I was born rich!

These fabulous songs will help change your patterns and attitude so you will attract a more positive and fulfilling lifestyle. Whether you exercise to her tape series or meditate to her Magnetic Creative Visualization Imaging tape, you'll begin to heal and cleanse! Before long, you can't help but change your thinking for the better, which will guide you to be the best *you* that you can possibly be. This will allow you to enjoy life in a completely new way.

Always remember…it's perfectly normal to *re-adjust*, fine-tune, and even change your dreams, goals, and visions along the way. Sometimes we envision or perceive our final destination to *look* a certain way, but in reality, when we finally arrive, it doesn't appear even *close* to what we thought it would look like. This is why it's always important to enjoy the journey. It's like *constructing your reality into existence* as you go.

If *what we say* really makes that much difference and I believe it does, then "affirming the positive" simply makes sense.

179

The following is one of my favorite affirmations. Feel free to adjust the words to fit your dreams, visions, and ultimate lifestyle:

"I, _____...am one of the most powerful people in the universe! People have respect for me wherever I go and wherever I am! My Intuition is always 'Right On!' I LOVE who I am! I am appropriate in ALL situations."

Affirmations are a powerful, dynamic way to liberate your soul *and* bring about permanent behavioral changes. Allow affirmations to become a part of you forever! It's how you rewrite your script for the new you!

I highly recommend you go to Michele's website and order her life-changing products at **www.MusiVation.com**. Her work is an absolute **must** for everyone's self-improvement library! Michele's material will continually contribute to your personal breakthroughs and accelerate your life in every way.

> *I am always living in determination*
> *That a certain outcome will emerge!*
> *I am always aiming with the intention*
> *That my dreams are not only coming true,*
> *But that they've already arrived,*
> *As if in the 3rd dimension!*
>
> - J'en El

Remember to review portions of this book
at least a few times every week!

Now that you know what to do, the only thing
that's left *is to take action and be happy!*

– References –

❏ To order Dr. Howard Peiper and Nina Anderson's book *"The Secrets of Staying Young"*, call...888-NATURE 1.

❏ To order USANA Health Science's Nutritional Supplements, Anti-Aging Skin Care, and Weight Loss products...
Or, call Lori Bell at: 801-954-7203.
Or, visit the website: www.FindingComfort.com
Or, leave a message on Voice Mail, 800-567-3602.

❏ To order Michele Blood's MusiVation Self-Help & Motivational products, go to: www.MusiVation.com and www.MpowerTV.com Or, call 800-547-5601.

❏ For information about Michael Adamson's workshops and presentations on *"The Power of Perception – Discovering a New Way of Being With Your Experience So That the Problems You've Been Struggling With and Trying to Overcome Begin to Spontaneously and Effortlessly Clear-Up in the Process of Everyday Living,"* call 888-304-6949. Or, send an email to: Adamson@san.rr.com

❏ To order Michael Adamson's book, *"Radical Insight: Re-Awakening To Your Always Already Present Condition of Wholeness, Serenity, and Well-Being,"* call 888-304-6949. Or, send an email to: Adamson@san.rr.com

❏ To order more copies of *"Finding Comfort In Your Own Skin"*, call 800-567-3602. Or, go to: www.FindingComfort.com